Alive Again

FINAL

SUNDAY ⊙ NEWS
NEW YORK'S PICTURE NEWSPAPER ®

25¢

Vol. 51. No. 27   Copr. 1971 New York News Inc.   New York, N.Y. 10017, Sunday, October 31, 1971*   WEATHER: Sunny, breezy and mild.

DAs SUBPENA
KNAPP RECORDS

Phillips Will Sing an Encore

—— Story on Page 3

Another False Step. Howard Samuels Jr., 19, (left), son of the offtrack betting chief, steps over wooden planking outside police precinct in Forest Hills, Queens, as he's taken with two other prisoners to night court. Arrested in 1969 on drug charge, he was nabbed at Kennedy Airport yesterday with 1½ bags of heroin. —*Story on page 3*

NEWS photo by Tom Monaster

Alive Again

RECOVERING FROM ALCOHOLISM AND DRUG ADDICTION

Howard C. Samuels, Psy.D.
with Jane O'Boyle

WILEY

Cover Design: John Wiley & Sons, Inc.
Cover Photograph: © Imagewerks/Getty Images

Published by John Wiley & Sons, Inc., Hoboken, New Jersey
Published simultaneously in Canada

The information contained in this book is not intended to serve as a replacement for professional medical advice. Any use of the information in this book is at the reader's discretion. The author and the publisher specifically disclaim any and all liability arising directly or indirectly from the use or application of any information contained in this book. A health care professional should be consulted regarding your specific situation.

For general information about our other products and services, please contact our Customer Care Department within the United States at (800) 762-2974, outside the United States at (317) 572-3993 or fax (317) 572-4002. For general information about our other products and services, please contact our Customer Care Department within the United States at (800) 762-2974, outside the United States at (317) 572-3993 or fax (317) 572-4002.

Wiley also publishes its books in a variety of electronic formats and by print-on-demand. Some content that appears in standard print versions of this book may not be available in other formats. For more information about Wiley products, visit us at www.wiley.com.

ISBN 978-1-118-36441-3 (hardcover); ISBN 978-1-118-52046-8 (ebk); ISBN 978-1-118-52057-4 (ebk); ISBN 978-1-118-52846-4 (ebk)

Printed in the United States of America

10 9 8 7 6 5 4 3 2 1

For the family who saved my life,
and for my new family, who gives me life.

Contents

A Note to Readers   ix

Acknowledgments   xi

Introduction   1

PART ONE   Identify the Problem

   1   The Story of My Addiction   13

   2   The Facts behind Alcoholism and
      Other Addictions   35

   3   Dealing with the Demon   48

   4   The Role of the Brain in Addiction   61

PART TWO   Recovery Solutions

   5   The Hills Recovery Program   77

   6   Fallback Addictions   90

   7   Shedding the Shame and Guilt   97

8   The Value of Support Groups   105

9   Working the 12 Steps   121

10   The Reality of Relapse   161

PART THREE   For Family and Friends

11   Taking Steps to Intervene   177

12   Healing the Whole Family   203

13   Advice for Parents   216

PART FOUR   Your Life Is a Gift

14   Service to Others and Yourself   231

15   The Grateful Life   241

Resources   250

Index   259

A Note to Readers

I have helped many alcoholics and addicts. My program is a model for you to follow with your own therapists and family members. I urge you to consult your own doctor or a professional therapist, many of whom can be found through the Resources at the end of this book.

Acknowledgments

I would not be alive today were it not for my brothers and sisters, William, Carey, Catherine, Vicky, Bobbi, Jacquie, and Janie. You never gave up hope for me, after all I put you through, and words cannot express what you mean to me. The same goes for my friends at Phoenix House, especially Mitch Rosenthal and my counselor, Lenny Copp.

This book would not have been created without the help and support of Amy Williams, Tom Miller, Connie Santisteban, and Jane O'Boyle. And every day I am helped in my sobriety and in my profession by my coworkers at the Hills Treatment Center, Bruce Turner and Jorja Davis. You have helped far more people than me, and your work will provide benefits for generations to come. I couldn't work with a finer collection of dedicated, caring people.

My beautiful wife, Gabrielle, and our children, Cooper, Greer, and Chase, are daily reminders of the greatest joys in life. You are supportive without fail, not only for me but for the rest of our community. I am so grateful to have you, and I love you more every day.

And deepest thanks to all the alcoholics and addicts I have met in twenty-eight years of sobriety. You are each a part of the community that keeps me on the path of recovery. You have made me who I am—you help me to stay sober, and to be grateful, every day.

Introduction

My parents were upstairs, having cocktails with their friends: the mayor of New York City, John Lindsay; Ted Kennedy; Christopher Dodd; Mario Cuomo; the usual crowd. My father was running for governor again in the New York state primary. A brilliant graduate of MIT, my dad had invented plastic Baggies and Hefty bags, worked for General George Patton in the war in Europe, then served as undersecretary of commerce for President Lyndon Johnson. We had moved to New York from Washington, D.C., and our family was renting a penthouse duplex that belonged to the Broadway star Mary Martin. My parents, siblings, and I shared the building with Greta Garbo and the Heinz family, among other well-to-do New Yorkers. The sunrise views over the East River were magnificent, and every room was filled with fine art. I remember that Ms. Martin owned many sculptures that depicted hands: wringing hands, open hands, marble hands that reached up from coffee tables, gold hands that prayed on bookshelves. My bedroom was on the lower floor, with an elegant bathroom that had walls covered in silk. The fabric was pale gray, printed with Chinese scenes, birds and flowers. I heard the tinkling of ice cubes and laughter upstairs, while I sat on the floor of the bathroom, a cigarette dangling from my lips. I had a needle in my arm, pushing it in and out—"booting" heroin

1

I'd just copped down in the East Village—rushing my brains out.
I was twenty, fresh off two arrests for drug possession, unemployed, misunderstood, a convicted felon, a junkie. But I owned
the fucking world. I pulled out the needle and loosened the tour-
niquet, feeling the relief enter my bloodstream. I could hear Ted
Kennedy's voice and my father serving more drinks upstairs. The
syringe in my hand glowed happy red, with some of my own
blood. I pressed my thumb hard, spraying blood all over the silk
wall fabric. In my world of darkness and destruction, that felt
pretty good.

I hit bottom again and again, for twelve more years after that.
Like all addicts, I would toe the line for a while but then relapse,
breaking my parents' hearts more times than I can count. If anyone was an incorrigible drug addict, it was me. I was an addict
who would forget that I was an addict, and I put on a terrific act.
I presented myself well, appearing quite articulate and friendly—
part of my enormous talent for manipulation. When I share my
horror stories of addiction now, with patients and their families,
they are surprised, but they nod their heads in recognition. They
also feel a little kernel of hope, because I have been sober now
for twenty-eight years. And if a dope fiend like me can recover
and live a normal life, so can you or your loved one.

After I became sober, I designed effective recovery programs
for rehabilitation centers. I have treated thousands of addicts and
alcoholics and have learned through experience what has proved
successful for recovery. This book encapsulates my program to
slay the beast of addiction. I wrote this book to help families who
have already identified that there is a problem with addiction—
whether it is you or another member of your family. Perhaps you
have a parent who spends every evening drinking a case of beer
or a son who's been arrested with a DUI. Your sister may be a
heroin addict, or your roommate stays up all night doing cocaine
and has stopped paying the rent. Maybe you have blackouts

when you drink and get into fights at bars or show up late to work one too many times. Maybe you've lost your savings by bailing out your brother, yet again. He's tried to quit and feels awful but has no control over his desire to use drugs. Perhaps you have just lost your job because you couldn't pass the company drug test.

There are times when recovery seems impossible. I've been there. I know. But I have dedicated my life in sobriety to implementing treatment programs that work. Although I have a doctorate in psychology, I gained the most expertise while struggling with my own addiction, until the age of thirty-two. That's where I learned that addicts are masters at lying and manipulation. Addiction is the one disease that will tell you that you don't have a disease. Addiction will lie to you: "I know I can't do cocaine anymore, but I can handle a little glass of scotch." "I have a good job, so what if I drink a bottle of wine every night?" "It's just a little weed; I've got everything under control."

The other challenge with this disease is that it is not eliminated by simple surgery or controlled by a pill. It is managed only by psychotherapy that is often traumatic—a 12-step program—followed by years of conscientious behavior. I have yet to see a patient who quits her addiction easily and quickly. She might make a good-faith effort, really work at it for a couple months, but then there will be an office party, and she'll believe she has learned how to control her addiction. She's still seeing her therapist. She's feeling all right, and it's only one drink; her issues aren't with alcohol anyway, it's only this one time. The addict thinks he is cleverer than other abusers of drugs and alcohol, that he will be the exception who can handle the issue by himself. He will believe with all his heart that he can make it on his own. Yet one thing always leads to another.

The landscape of addiction is different today than it used to be, and I work with this changed environment every day. Avenues to addiction appear for kids at a younger and younger age. Now,

there is also a higher level of acceptance for drinking and drugging. Kids bypass old-fashioned high school drinking and go
straight to snorting OxyContin, which is easily available in many
medicine cabinets. Prescription drugs such as Vicodin, Xanax,
Percocet, and Ambien have enormously increased our addict
population. We know marijuana is addicting, and now even more
so when it is legally prescribed by a medical doctor (at least, in
California), not for cancer or epilepsy but for "anxiety." Heroin
and crack are cheaper than ever. Adderall is an amphetamine
that teens love to use to help them study or to lose weight.
Cocaine is even more prevalent—we see young celebrities
emerge from criminal convictions unscathed, unremorseful, and
still addicted. In addition to the run-of-the-mill narcotics, we
have an alarming number of new drugs, some of which cause
lasting brain damage: crystal meth, "bath salts," Ecstasy, salvia,
and who knows what will be invented tomorrow?

What hasn't changed is this: the nature of addiction. The
need to use, self-medicate, and self-destruct is the manifestation
of an inner "beast." It's the part of us that tells us, "You're stupid,"
"Your parents don't want you," or "You will never fit in." We all
have that beast inside us, whether we're addicts or not. Many of
you can cope with that dark, negative part of your persona—or
ignore it—and not succumb to the seduction of drugs or alcohol.
But for those who are coming of age or living in dysfunctional
family situations, keeping up with sophisticated peer groups,
insecure, unemployed, clinically depressed, or genetically predis-
posed to addiction in the first place, well, your disease is going to
win round one.

The disease is emotional emptiness, lack of self-esteem or
personal fulfillment, and it's why we drink and do drugs. We are
numbing ourselves to loneliness, fear, alienation, emotional or
physical abuse, isolation, or self-doubt. Of course, many people
have these conditions and do not become addicts. They cope

with their demons in other ways. Yet more and more people are relying on drugs and alcohol.

One recent study from Phoenix House (where I spent two years in rehab) attributes our current rise in addiction rates to the recent economic turndown, reflecting a further devastating impact on individuals, families, and entire communities. According to this study, 34 percent of respondents have a friend or a family member who is currently struggling with substance abuse, and 40 percent say that drugs have caused trouble in their families at some point. About a third of the respondents reported more drinking and more drug use since the financial turndown on the part of friends, coworkers, and family members. There seem to be even more "reasons" for people to medicate themselves on a daily basis. Many of us seem unable to be comfortable in our own skin. A recent study estimated that 20 million Americans age twelve and over are in need of addiction treatment and are not receiving it. Unfortunately, even the majority of people who *do* seek out treatment will fail.

Alcoholics and addicts are hitting bottom much faster—in their twenties, instead of their forties—and that can be seen as good news, in one respect. With addicts at younger ages, families can intervene more quickly. Helping an addict who is still young gives him or her a greater chance of success. The addict is not as experienced at manipulation and lying, which someone like me had years to perfect. Twenty, thirty years of addictive behavior is harder to change. Some of us older addicts are the victims of our "happy hour" traditions and Western standards in medicine, where we sometimes treat not the cause of our ailments but only the symptoms with remedies such as Vicodin, Xanax, and Ambien.

The other good news is that we have more community awareness of the issue and of the challenges to successful recovery and more facilities and professionals who provide effective treatment.

In 2012, the standard reference book for psychiatric disorders expanded its definition of addiction to include not only substance abuse and alcoholism, but also behavioral addictions such as sex and gambling. This means that more medical experts understand the evolving areas and challenges of what can trigger the pleasure impulses in our brains, to the extent that these triggers can damage our lives.

I draw upon my own experiences, as well as on case studies from my clients and coworkers, because I know many of you will relate to them. There are few, if any, books about recovery that come from a therapist who has also been an addict. It is my experience that patients respond more to therapists who they know have been to that same hell where they are living. Each of us has a unique story, but every story illustrates that you can reach that authentic self inside you who is waiting to be found. She's hiding behind that inner beast that fills you with self-doubt and rage.

This book is a step-by-step guide for finding help, whether you are an addict or you have a loved one who is. If a family member is an addict, you are basically the only one who can help save that person. I explain why many addicts and alcoholics behave the way they do and what are the best things you can do to heal yourself and your family. I help you understand the root causes of this disease and the best steps you can take toward recovery. This involves healing for the whole family, because everyone suffers when there's an addict in the family, whether it is you, your child, your spouse, your sibling, or your parent.

In *Alive Again*, I describe the nature of addiction, first by telling you my story and the stories of people I work with. I describe how the disease works at tearing down each of us and why addiction can frequently be the easiest way to cope with the beast. I include a chapter on groundbreaking studies about the role of brain development, particularly in the frontal lobe. Our brains are still developing until age twenty-two (for girls) and age twenty-six (for boys), and when dopamine and serotonin confront changing hormones and unreliable social environments, you have recipes for disaster.

A patient cannot begin recovery until he or she has hit bottom. Most clients I see have yet to reach that point; in fact, many are still drugging and drinking while they're in therapy with me. There was once a time when people thought shaming someone in a boot-camp environment would hasten the patient to reach bottom. I have learned that doesn't really work: a patient will say and do anything to appear compliant and to avoid painful confrontation. I know that addicts have dual natures—one bent on self-destruction and negativity, and one that dreams of peace and happiness. Therapy is useful only when patients have moved beyond shame, when they're no longer embarrassed to admit they have a problem and need help. This usually occurs when they hit bottom, often after landing in jail or in a hospital. I try to convince the patients that I am on their side, to help them do battle against their disease, and that I will be with them every step of the way. While the patient and I form a team to fight anger, delusion, and addiction, I also try to help this individual form a sense of self-respect and an engagement with real life. Sometimes, parents think that money, a new car, or a place to live will bring their children happiness and sobriety. In fact, those things only cause the addiction to become worse. I so often see kids and adults who have what I call the "Disease of More." There's just never enough money or love, or power or career success or fame. Then there's never enough booze or drugs.

Chapter 5 is dedicated to finding an effective therapist and determining what his or her role is in the rehab process. I also detail the specific programs that we implement at the Hills, our California rehabilitation center, and offer facts about each type of addiction, as well as consider the mental conditions and the living situation for the patient. I do not recommend that you or your family act as your own therapists—you should always turn to a professional. *Alive Again* is a guide that explains the options and the processes, and that outlines the best chances for success.

Part of my therapy program prepares you for the arrival of a "new" addiction. As a fallback, many addicts turn to cigarettes or sex or even sitting in a dark room playing video games all day. I walk you through the work on removing the shame and the guilt that drive these compulsions. Although *Alive Again* is not in itself a 12-step guide, I explain why 12-step programs work, how to find them, and what other additional steps lead to success in recovery.

One hallmark in the 12-step group philosophy is not only community support but also providing service to others, which is actually service to yourself. After several years of sobriety, I never understood what it meant to have a "higher power." One day I was working as a counselor for Phoenix House in New York City, sitting on a stoop on the Upper West Side with a sixteen-year-old addict. He was dying to go out to get loaded, filled with anger at his parents and resentment of society, and looking for reasons why it was okay for him to go out and score drugs. I'd been there; I knew exactly how he felt. I talked to him for maybe half an hour, right there on West 74th Street, and, at least that day, he did not go get high. It was the first time since I'd been sober that I felt some fucking self-worth. This young man had broken down and admitted his fears and his insecurities. To be a part of that process while he opened up emotionally was a very spiritual experience for me. I'd failed at school and never had a career path, but at that moment I knew my calling was to help others in the community. That was my "higher power." That was my authentic self.

I went to rehab twice. The first time it didn't take. As I mentioned, relapse is part of recovery—if you make it back alive. At least, we have recognized the disease, which is a huge step. Falling off the wagon is par for the course. In my case, relapse lasted more than a decade. Finally, in my early thirties, I entered Phoenix House and stayed for two years. I was locked up in treatment centers for close to three years and have worked on developing rehab programs for more than twenty years. I have lived it, breathed it, and loved it. I have also had success in treating other addicts. I'm still crazy. I'm just "good crazy," not bad crazy. And that's what I want for you and your loved one.

My success with patients is largely due to the therapists at the Hills, the people I work with who are all recovering addicts. Like me, their personal experiences help make them good at helping others. The clients connect with these counselors, respect them, and understand that they, too, have been to hell and back. *Alive Again* is filled with their stories and mine, and scores of others, because it helps a patient to hear another addict's story. Working in Hollywood, I have treated many a "celebrity," and anecdotes about them—and most of the case studies in this book—are heavily disguised. Their stories are no different than yours. Money and fame do not make sobriety any easier, trust me. The delusional drunk in Detroit is as angry and spiritually empty as the schoolteacher in Dallas. It would help if our society stopped worshiping money and redefined the American Dream to focus more on helping other people. Working in a soup kitchen or tutoring kids after school can bring rewards of personal connection that can replace our desires for drugs and alcohol or any addiction. When you truly engage in community and caring for others, it is easy to conquer the self-doubt and say, "Fuck you, Beast! I am better than you say I am."

We are born sober. We are supposed to live our lives sober. We are not meant to numb our bodies or our brains. Who are you that you need to smoke weed every day? Who are you that you continue to hurt people who love you? Who are you that this world is not good enough? You have helping hands all around you, and, still, you are someone who is missing a human connection. According to the annual study from the National Center on Addiction and Substance Abuse at Columbia University, if a person reaches the age of twenty-one without smoking, using drugs, or abusing alcohol, that person is virtually certain never to become addicted. The study also confirms that no one has more power than a parent does when it comes to a teen's decision to drink or to use drugs. Our goal, then, is to start the young on the path to self-fulfillment, while letting them keep their individuality—to become good crazy.

Even if you are an older patient, you can be better, with the knowledge in this book, with love, therapy, and the great community of people—including myself—who know you can succeed. It does take a village to help someone who is in the throes of addiction. We must all do our part. Remember that life is sweeter when you live the way you were meant to live, when you come into your authentic self, coping with everyday challenges and truly enjoying the moments of fulfillment and happiness that await you.

PART ONE

*Identify
the
Problem*

I

The Story of
My Addiction

My father was a remarkable man. He came from modest means but graduated from MIT, where he wrote his thesis, "The Manufacturing and Distribution Problems of Vinyl-Coated Sisal Rope as a Clothesline." Basically, he invented a number of household uses for a new technology known as plastic. After college, he served in World War II as a lieutenant colonel on General George Patton's staff. His responsibility was managing fuel supplies for the 130,000 Allied tanks across Europe, where he eventually took part in liberating concentration camps. After the war, my dad started Kordite, a company that went on to create Baggies and Hefty bags.

I was the fifth child of Howard and Barbara Samuels, who had eight kids. In 1958, when I was five, my father sold his company to Mobil Oil for $43 million, which today would be equivalent to half a billion dollars. My father then entered the world of public service. He was undersecretary of commerce for President Lyndon Johnson, director of the Small Business Administration, and chairman of the Democratic National Committee, and he ran for governor of New York several times. My mother, who was an actress before she met my father, stood by his side throughout, the epitome of a political wife. They employed a succession of cooks and housekeepers to raise the children, much in the mold of the Kennedys.

We lived on a three-hundred-acre estate in Canandaigua, New York, at the end of a long and looping tree-lined driveway, in a huge brick house that had been built in the 1800s. One of the groundskeepers usually drove us to school. Although my parents frequently traveled, they made a point of having picture-perfect family dinners. The ten of us sat in the formal dining room, elbows off the table. Mother rang a bell to summon the servants carrying trays of food, and Father would ask each of us a question that, all during my young life, filled me with dread: "What did you do today to be productive?"

My brother and sisters always had impressive answers. They were all straight-A students and went on to attend prestigious universities. I was a horrible student. I hated to read, got lousy grades, and spent a lot of time watching TV. My father declared I was lazy, but, in reality, I was dyslexic in the era before anyone had ever identified this learning disability. I struggled in reading and writing, and any attempt by my dad to help me always ended in a screaming fight. Maybe this situation sounds familiar to some of you. Of course, it was natural for me to conclude that I was stupid and, as my parents always assured me, that I would never amount to much in life. As I grew older, less and less was expected of me.

"People made allowances for you," a family friend once told me. I became an angry and lonely kid. My older brother Bill was a star student. I was close to my sisters, but they all went away to boarding school, and I was left largely on my own. My parents became more and more involved with my father's political career. Mom's priorities were focused entirely on Dad. On a family vacation in Paris, we kids were stunned to hear my mother declare, "Your father comes first. I love you children, but he is my life." When my parents came home from their travels, my father was usually exhausted and headed straight to the sofa for a nap. Once in a while, we went to Sunday services at the local Congregationalist church.

I had no self-confidence or self-esteem and no one to talk to about my feelings. I seemed to get into fights at school almost every day. One day, I fouled a kid on the basketball court.

"Jew boy!" he shouted at me. I slugged him.

When I got home and told this to my father, he paused and then said, "Son, I've got news for you."

Dad revealed that he was, in fact, Jewish—yet another obfuscation of identity on my way to adulthood.

My grades were so low that it was difficult to find a school that would admit me. I went to a boarding school named Allendale in upstate Rochester, New York. I had about a D average, and I remember how it killed me to hear the headmaster tell my father, "For Howard, this is pretty good."

The boarding school was in a rural area, and all of us students spent a large part of our day drinking beer and smoking pot. No hard drugs were around, thankfully. I had long hair and worked at being as cool as possible—as hip as a fourteen-year-old can be. I remember meeting Robert F. Kennedy around this time. He was running for the Senate in New York and relied on my father's political connections in the state, because Kennedy was actually from Massachusetts. When I shook Bobby Kennedy's hand the first time I met him, he laughed and said, "You look just like my sheepdog!"

My father ran unsuccessfully for governor of New York in 1966. The following year, when he was named undersecretary of commerce by President Lyndon Johnson, my family moved to Washington, D.C. We were all very proud of my dad, and he was happy about his appointment. We leased a house in the district, and my parents began to search for a new high school. This was excruciating for me because, once again, my shortcomings and inadequacies were moved into the spotlight, in hopes that a school somewhere would accept me. My father prevailed on his friend Hubert H. Humphrey—then vice president of the United States—who wrote me a letter of recommendation; I managed to gain entrance into Maret School.

At Maret, I learned the fine art of using hard-core narcotics. My dad had given me a car, which made me very popular with my fellow students. My friend Dave liked to ride around D.C. with me. It turned out that Dave was a drug dealer, so I drove him to make his deliveries. I was already an avid pot smoker, but my friend had all sorts of other things in his pockets: cocaine, heroin, a syringe, a spoon. One evening, we drove to Dave's parents' house, which was as beautiful as my own.

"You want to try some?" he asked.

"Absolutely!" I said, without hesitation. Dave showed me how to tie off, and I stuck the needle in. That speedball hit me, and I never felt anything so amazing in my life. Every bad feeling I ever had disappeared. I was sixteen, and I was off and running.

I hung out in Georgetown with Dave and a bunch of other rich private school students. Every day of the week, I shot heroin, snorted coke, dropped acid, or smoked pot—and sometimes all of the above. Although this was the "hippie" era of peace and love, we weren't hippies. We were prep-school drug addicts, angry and destructive. My buddies and I called ourselves "Nazi

Maoist Anarchist Nihilists." Whatever you had, we were against it. We were young and privileged, and we wanted to burn down everything. We attended every political demonstration we could, antsy to throw the first rock or smash the first window. I loved living in D.C. then, with buses surrounding the White House, machine guns on rooftops, the constant threat of violence in the air. We were merely surviving, with a gaping void in our lives, without a connection to anything meaningful. Our only connection to each other was our shared addiction to drugs of any kind.

In 1968, Dad was a delegate to the Democratic National Convention in Chicago, and the whole family tagged along. For three days, while Dad was at the convention, I was on the streets pumped up on Black Beauties—speed, that is, the precursor to today's methamphetamines. I was a raving fanatic, falling in with assorted street gangs, breaking windows, burning trash, cursing out cops, trying to turn cars over. It felt glorious. I was no Bobby Seale or Abbie Hoffman, protesting the war machine. I was a punk having a good time. Until I was tear-gassed, pepper-sprayed, and eventually arrested and thrown into a holding pen. The whole family came to bail me out. Dad even brought John Byrnes, the head of the New York State Democratic Party. These influential representatives started to negotiate with the desk sergeant to post not only my bail but the bail of everyone who was arrested with me. While I waited with my mother, I rubbed my eye with my hand, which still had pepper spray on it. Tears flooded my eyes, and I remember my mother wailing loudly at the police station: "What have they done to my son? What have they done to my son?"

Oddly enough, I could tell that my father was a little proud of me during that incident. He thought I'd been arrested because I was actively participating in something I cared about, that I was showing a sense of commitment to a cause, a quality that he respected in people. It wasn't his fault, but his pride was certainly misplaced, because I didn't give a shit about anything. My inner beast had spent years telling me, "You are stupid. You will never be as good or as successful as other people." Yet I was learning that there was one thing I enjoyed, one thing I was good at. My goal in life was to become a major drug dealer.

Life in the Big Apple

In 1969, Richard M. Nixon moved into the White House, and my dad was out of a job. The family moved to New York City, while my father prepared to run for governor again. That's when we rented the apartment on East 52nd Street that belonged to Mary Martin. She was known around the world for creating the singing roles of the century, starring in Broadway musicals such as *South Pacific*, *The Sound of Music*, and *Peter Pan*. She was living in Brazil at the time, so we moved into the exquisitely furnished apartment overlooking the East River. By then, I was a senior in high school and had been accepted for my final year at the Dwight School on East 69th Street. My father was completely occupied, deliberating whether to enter the governor's race, and my mother was by his side at every function, so they were never home. All of my siblings were overachieving at Sarah Lawrence and Harvard and Columbia. I was virtually on my own, and New York City was my new playground.

Downtown in the East Village was a great place to score drugs. One night, a few weeks into the school year, I bought some hash behind Cooper Union. Next thing I knew, four guys in plain clothes flashed police badges and shouted, "Up against the wall!" They searched my pockets and found some Tuinals, which were great sleeping pills in the days before Ambien, and the hashish I had bought. It was amazing I wasn't carrying anything more—thankfully, I was fresh out of coke and smack. I was handcuffed and taken to the Ninth Precinct on East 5th Street.

I spent about four hours there, called my parents, and everything was cool until my father's prick of a lawyer arrived. He was sarcastic with me, which ignited my own fury and "fuck you" attitude. I was quite the hothead.

Back at home, my parents were concerned but relatively sympathetic and caring. I put on a good show of contrition, reassuring them that I wasn't into hard drugs. The next day, the headmaster at Dwight put his arm around my shoulder and said, "Son, let's just keep this between ourselves."

A few weeks later, my father officially entered the race for governor. He'd lost the same race in 1966, but his supporters were certain that 1970 would be his year. In January, when I showed up in court with Mom and Dad to answer for my run-of-the-mill misdemeanor, the media circus showed up, too. At that time, it was extremely rare for a noteworthy person to be associated with a drug arrest, so my little story landed in the *New York Times*, in *Time*, in *Newsweek*, and on the front page of the *New York Daily News*. Stories about celebrity-related drug arrests were so rare that it even rated a piece in my favorite magazine, *Rolling Stone*. I had given a press statement and told the court, "I made a big mistake, and I'm sorry I caused all this trouble."

I was considered a youthful offender and was given probation. After my photo appeared in the newspapers, I was recognized on the streets for days. But this time when I went back to Dwight, the headmaster did not put his arm around my shoulder. It was no longer "just between us." In fact, I was no longer welcome on school property but would be tutored at home, though I still would be able to get a diploma. That didn't bother me in the least, because I didn't really believe I'd made a mistake and wasn't sorry at all.

My father lost the governor's race in the 1970 primary (to Arthur Goldberg, who ultimately lost to Nelson Rockefeller). Yet he made plans to run again in 1974, so I spent the next couple of years in a dual life: working on my dad's gubernatorial race by day and partying at night, doing a whole lot of hard drugs. This was the era of *Gimme Shelter*, Woodstock, Led Zeppelin, *A Clockwork Orange*, Quaaludes, psychedelic moon landings, Muhammad Ali, LSD, marijuana, Hank Aaron, American bombings in Cambodia, and heroin. I often brought total strangers home to the Mary Martin penthouse to shoot dope with. I remember one guy, Joe—a cab driver. When he wouldn't wake up in the morning, I carried him downstairs and threw him in the passenger seat. I got into his cab and drove around Manhattan for a while, picking up fares while Joe nodded off. When I got tired of it, I parked the taxi and left him in the front seat, still nodding.

I shot up heroin just about every day, endlessly listening and nodding off to "Sister Morphine," while my parents hosted political bigwigs upstairs. One night—well, early morning—I fell asleep with a cigarette and set my bedroom on fire. My mother and sisters and I ran down the fire stairs into the street. The fire department arrived and evacuated the entire building. Greta Garbo and all of our other neighbors stood outside on the sidewalk. When I saw Garbo, I realized I had forgotten to bring my sunglasses down. Like the faded movie star, I usually wore shades, day and night. As we milled around in the cold morning, waiting for the all clear, I heard one of the Heinzes mutter, "I'll bet it was that Samuels kid."

Later that night, I was back partying at Max's Kansas City, a nightclub on Park Avenue South where artists hung out: Andy Warhol, Patti Smith, Robert Mapplethorpe. The band was usually the Velvet Underground, and I got to be friends with Candy Darling, Anton Perich, John Waters, Fran Lebowitz, and Richard Powers. A group of us might stop and get a bite to eat at One Waverly Place, Mickey Ruskin's other place.

We took turns seeing which of us could seduce Ellen Barkin, who was a waitress there at the time. But we didn't have a chance. Afterward, we headed to the West Side meatpacking district, where streetwalkers, transvestites, and overall sexual behavior beggared the imagination. I was usually a voyeur, except when it came to getting high. I was a full-blown participant in any and all drugs available in this underbelly of the city. I loved living at the extreme edge and reveling in my fun-loving dark side: shooting heroin in Alphabet City (also known as the East Village), snorting coke in the clubs, shouting, "Fuck you!" in the streets at no one in particular. On any given day, I was up for anything. Actually, it was more like, up for everything.

My parents had no clue. It wasn't their fault, though; no one's parents had a clue in 1971. Most people (certainly not people like my parents) had no experience with drugs or even knew people who used them. My dad was basically gone most of the time, now that he was chairman of the Off-Track Betting Corporation and organizing his next political campaign. My mother usually drank some cocktails, took a pill (barbiturates didn't count as drugs!), and waited at our beautiful apartment for Dad to come home. My siblings were all at Columbia, MIT, and Harvard by then, and I was well on the way to my dream career as a drug dealer.

To be able to afford my heroin use, I started selling marijuana. One day, a customer called Mary Martin's apartment to complain about the half pound of pot I'd sold him, which had been a little light. I told him to come over and collect the rest.

My father was listening on the extension, furious, and wasted no time in confronting me. I'd never seen him react this way.

"As long as you live under my roof! You have to obey my rules! And obey the law! No doing drugs in this home! And no selling drugs, ever!" This was the first time my father had ever spoken to me with such anger. It actually frightened me a little.

"Okay, okay, no problem," I said, shaken. Then he shocked me.

"Although, on a positive note," he said, "I'm glad you're making good on your deals with your customers. You could be a good businessman." I was stunned by his naiveté about my drug use and also by his good intentions, his desperation to find something positive in a son who was beyond his understanding. More than that, I was greatly relieved, because had he at that moment chosen to search my bedroom, he would have found a great deal more than marijuana.

Naturally, I had been rejected by pretty much every college I had applied to. Yet once again, family connections got me into little Southampton College on Long Island. This place had a reputation among wealthy families for taking in any son or daughter, no matter how little promise they showed or how low a grade-point average they had. My fellow students at Southampton in 1971 were rich kids who would get a last-chance degree and move on to a do-nothing job in the family business. It was a beautiful campus near the beach, with carefree hippie students playing Frisbee all day. I supplied all of them with plenty of heroin, and, before long, they were more strung out than ever.

My disease was fully in control of everything I did, but I became bored with the scene of wealthy white dopeheads. I needed to be closer to the edge. Rather than attempt to go to any classes, I continued to pursue my dream of dealing drugs on a larger scale. Why not? My father was a brilliant industrialist, the former commerce undersecretary who had even, once or twice, admired my moxie. It was time for me to go global, to claim my destiny as an international drug lord. I made a plan to leave Long Island and set up shop in Afghanistan.

Then, as now, narcotics abounded in the land of the poppy. Morphine dripped like rain on Afghan streets, where no one arrested you and the drugs were pure as could be. I had a friend who worked in the post office in Kabul. I had another friend in New York who was eager for me to supply him with shit to sell on the streets. How hard could it be? Well, first I needed a little seed money. To raise some cash, I decided to make a small sale to the citizens in Boulder, Colorado. My sister Vicki was going to school there, and I had visited her a time or two. We had shared a little Centennial State pot smoking, she and I. When I made the trip to visit Vicki, I had invested about a thousand dollars in two ounces of cocaine and a few bags of smack to sell when I got there. On the return trip, I would be carrying back a hundred pounds of newly purchased pot. The proceeds of this Colorado adventure would fund my start-up in Afghanistan. I bought a plane ticket to the Mile High City.

I showed up at Kennedy Airport on an October morning, my pockets stuffed with drugs. There I was, in a sports coat and blue jeans, long hair to my shoulders, eyes pinned, totally high on heroin. My bulging pockets evidently drew the attention of two air marshals. As I waited in line to get on the plane, I felt them take my elbow and pull me to the side. A bag of coke practically felt out of my pants pocket, and I went ballistic with indignation. Inside, I was freaking out, but on the outside I was all anger and attitude. They escorted me to a private room off the concourse. The security officers searched my pockets and found more coke, ten bags of heroin, some speed, a map of Afghanistan, and a phone number in Kabul. I gave them shit with my "fuck you" attitude. They called the cops in Queens.

So I was arrested again and spent twenty-four hours in lockup. I had long survived on my anger and bravado, never having learned anything else to use as coping skills. When I was finally bailed out, the cameras and the reporters were waiting in the parking lot; I wore my dark shades, still steaming with anger.

By the time I got home to my parents' apartment, however, that attitude was gone. I was overwhelmed by shame and guilt for fucking up again, for fucking up before, for fucking up always. I walked into a room where my dad was conferring with a group of political advisers. Damage control was in full-scale operation. How would they handle this news, again, and what would they do about me this time? What would this mean for his future? And mine? I looked into my dad's eyes.

"I'm sorry," was all I could say.

"I don't care about me, Howard," he said, to my surprise. "All I care about is you."

In that moment, I allowed a real connection between him and me, and I will always remember that sensation. Until then I had spent years feeling only anger, shame, and frustration. Looking back, I can see that my arrogance covered up the feeling that I was a total fuck-up. My father knew otherwise, and I could see that, but he and I were in a moment in time when neither of us knew what to do about my mystifying behavior. It was comforting to feel that connection with him. It didn't last, of course. I had been without dope for more than twenty-four hours, and I was getting sick. I went out that night and scored some dope.

In the days that followed, I took a leave from college and convinced my parents to let me stay with Vicki in Boulder, while I awaited trial. Vicki reassured them that the clean mountain air would be good for me. God bless my sister. She helped me kick the heroin, once I got out West. There wasn't a protocol for withdrawal back in those days—it was simply straight-up five days of excruciating pain. But I made it, and I stayed off heroin the whole time I was in Colorado. I did plenty of coke and acid, though. Plenty of weed, too. But I was "clean." I let my hair grow long, to my shoulders, and I was rather proud of how that looked. However, I knew

I should appear in court with short hair. These were felony charges, not the misdemeanor I'd had earlier. So I bought a wig and shoved my long hair under it. When I flew home the day before the trial, my mother was overjoyed when she saw me.

"You look so good!" she said. "So clean cut!"

I smiled. The game was working. Since I'd been out of town for a few weeks and with a big day yet to come, I decided to go out and party that night. Score two more for my beast. When Dad woke me up at seven the next morning, to get ready for court, he looked at me with curiosity before leaving the room. I stood up and glanced in the mirror. The wig had fallen off, and my head was covered with the crooked mesh hairnet. I restored my short-hair wig and got dressed. In the car on the way to the courthouse, my parents and I were joined by a couple of my dad's political aides. One of them spotted a stray strand of hair hanging on my shoulder.

"Are you wearing a wig?" he asked.

"Uh-huh," I said.

My father exploded. "What the hell do you think you're doing?!" he shouted at me. "How much more can we tolerate your weird behavior?"

He had a right to be pissed, of course. I'd gotten busted— again—and gone out partying the night before, again, and here I was, trying to pull one over on a federal judge by pretending to have normal-length hair.

As usual, Dad was succinct in his expression, if clueless to the reality or its solution. He was a great man, a good guy, and I know how hard he tried to be a good father to me. He didn't have the tools to understand me any more than I did. In that era, people of my parents' generation had no knowledge of emotional or psychological issues—and neither did my own generation. I think back now about how such a brilliant engineer and states- man as my father must have been extraordinarily frustrated by my "weird behavior." He'd been repeatedly disappointed in me, his own namesake, the lazy student, the drug user, the law-breaker. Riding in the car that morning, I saw how guilty he felt, because of me. He blamed himself.

The judge blamed Dad, too. He used the media presence to grandstand and criticize Dad for using political influence to get me off the first time I had been arrested. Although I had not received any favorable treatment during earlier arrests, this dec-laration almost appeared to be a publicity stunt by one of Dad's political rivals. In fact, some people believed that my arrest itself was planned to foil the campaign of a "rich, Jewish, liberal Dem-ocrat." My parents had found listening devices in their apartment on more than one occasion, during Dad's campaigns. Maybe one of Dad's political rivals knew I was going to the airport that day. Yet even if that were true, I certainly made their work easy. Dur-ing my trial, I learned that the rationale JFK Airport security used to pull me out of line and search me was that I fit the profile of a "potential hijacker"—whatever that was.

Doing Time, Round One

I was convicted, and my sentence provided two options: four years in prison or one year in a drug rehabilitation center. Nat-urally, I chose the latter. I checked into a program called "Encounter," located in SoHo, which was still a relatively rough neighborhood of warehouses, sewing factories, and artists' lofts. Right off the bat, I learned a few hard lessons. First, that my survival "tools" of anger and attitude were not going to work in that place. Second, that I would not have any say in how things were done, and I was the one who would have to change. I also learned that I had to stop blaming other people for my troubles—stop blaming my dad, my mom, Richard Nixon, and everyone else in the universe. I hit rock bottom for the first time at Encounter, and I had to learn how to live life without being angry. It was like learning to walk and talk for the first time.

I will admit that it was enormously helpful to learn how to express my feelings in a healthy way. Being able to tell someone "I am hurt" or "I feel angry" enabled me to release that feeling to the universe, and then I could easily let it go. I started to feel less isolated, which brought a sense of peace and connection with other people. Sometimes it can be painful to confront your feelings and other people. We might do drugs or stay in bad relationships merely to avoid that confrontation. Some people believe that avoiding pain is better than reaching peace, but I learned that even drugs and alcohol don't relieve pain as much as the simple act of expressing it. It's funny that I had grown up with every advantage, from private school to home tutoring, but it was a drug rehab center that taught me how to communicate. It just goes to show that money and arrogance can go hand in hand in deceiving us about who we really are.

One year later, I was released clean and sober, and I enrolled in New York University (the admissions department liked my story of coping with a learning disability and drug addiction). I studied film and earned solid Bs in my courses. I got my first girlfriend, and I actually graduated and got a good job, making industrial films. I made new friends and rented my own apartment. Things were finally going in my favor, although I still wasn't very happy. Once in a while, I'd have a beer or two. Of course, we know now that it's all the same slippery slope. At the time, though, no one thought there was any connection between alcohol and drug addiction. So I'd have a beer now and then.

Yet by the late 1970s, cocaine was everywhere in New York City. I mean, everywhere. I had friends—assistant district attorneys and other professionals—who would do a few lines now and again and then not touch the stuff for months. I admired that. I'd

always avoided the coke at parties, but after months of watching
other people do it with no ill effects, I started rationalizing to
myself. My real problem had been heroin, not cocaine. Everyone
else seemed to do coke from time to time, with no repercussions.
Early transgressions make it easier and easier to achieve new
ones. I started saying yes to a line, here and there. It was such a
tremendous rush at first. Then, of course, it made me hyper and
sleepless, so I'd pop a Valium or a Percocet to calm myself down.
I did more coke, a lot of it, and needed something stronger to
bring me down from it. So I started in on the opiates. One day, I
rationalized that it would be okay to snort a little heroin. I told
myself that my problems were with shooting it, not snorting it. I
did a little rationalizing whenever I had an opportunity to do
more drugs, and after a couple of years I was back in the belly of
the beast.

I got bored with my job making industrial films, so I quit and
took a job as a doorman for the Roxy, a huge roller disco in
Chelsea. What a scene! It was a chaotic circus of celebrities, sex,
drugs, and rock and roll, and I was at the center of it all. Drugs
were everywhere, and I handed them out like party favors. When
we celebrated the victory of the 1980 U.S. Olympic Hockey
team, I gave everyone gifts of cocaine, and then went to after-
parties with off-duty cops who worked security, providing the
coke for everyone. I started to visit the clientele during the day
at their offices. I remember the rock impresario Bill Graham
imploring me to stop with the drugs. I ignored him. I was back in
the clutches of addiction.

In 1979, I went to a party at Vice President Walter Mondale's
historic home at the U.S. Naval Observatory. The house was
filled with foreign dignitaries and state leaders getting drunk. I
went into one of the bathrooms at the mansion, to shoot heroin.
When I emerged, loaded out of my mind, I walked right up to the
vice president, who was a friend of my dad's.

"Hey! How are you doing?" I proceeded to have a five-minute conversation with Vice President Mondale, which I don't remember very well. When Senator Ted Kennedy ran for president in the Democratic primary of 1980, my family connections secured me a gig doing advance work for a campaign event in New York City. I went to the venue a week before the event, which was at Windows on the World, high atop the World Trade Center. I worked with guys from the Secret Service, met with coordinators, talked to employees, and checked out the elevators and the private rooms. On the night of the event, I met Kennedy at the elevator and briefed him about who was there, and I escorted him to the right place. That night, as I had been the entire week, I was high on cocaine. I would sneak off to the john and snort a line, then go back out to talk with Kennedy.

There's nothing worse than coming off a cocaine high, so you do just about as much as you can to keep the high going. Highs could be sublime, of course, but after I did coke for seventy-two hours, my heart started to race and my head felt as if it were about to explode. One time, I thought I was going to die, and I called an ambulance. I also called my sister Vicki, who lived nearby at the time, and she came running down the street, sobbing, as emergency technicians wheeled me outside. The EMTs stabilized my heartbeat, and I went home to recover. While I was in bed, I overheard Vicki calling our siblings to discuss my "situation." I felt sick to my stomach, listening to her. I was so ashamed and guilt-ridden. When I got well, I swore to all of them that I wouldn't touch cocaine again. Then I went back on heroin.

My father had, by then, divorced my mother and married a Parisienne whose father had once been the prime minister of France. I was running with Chinese gang members in the East Village, smoking crack in Tompkins Square Park, and scoring heroin in Alphabet City. It was a constant adventure, and I loved the rush of living on the edge once again. I tried to get a new job

after the Roxy closed. My dad got me an interview with HBO
Films through Michael Fuchs, his old friend. I showed up with
coke all over my nose. I didn't get the job.

On more than one occasion, I encountered John Belushi at
my dealer's house on Barrow Street, in the West Village. The
comedian was at the peak of his career, on the heels of *Saturday
Night Live*. Of course, he was there for the same reason I was.
He and I would hang around the dealer's place and snort a few
lines together. We were about the same age, and we certainly had
similar addictions. Within a year or two, Belushi would be dead
from an overdose.

I started stealing from my girlfriend and would rifle through
coat pockets at parties on the Upper East Side. I'd go visit my
mother, now living alone on Park Avenue, and steal from her
purse and her medicine cabinet while she anesthetized herself
with pills. I still remember her expression whenever she opened
the front door for me: the look on her face was fear, fear of her
own son. After I lost my apartment, I moved in with her. She and
I separately medicated ourselves, alone in our respective rooms.
One morning, I'd been up all night doing coke, and I took a
Valium to bring me down. I had one line left, though, not enough
to really carry me back up. So I took a razor blade and slit open
the skin on my left shoulder. I took the last of the coke and
rubbed it into this gaping wound. I later woke up in a mass of
bloody sheets, truly in the thrall of my beast.

One night I went out to dinner with my father and three of
my sisters. They had consulted a drug intervention specialist and
that night announced to me that the family was going to cut me
off—no money, no contact, no nothing. I desperately did not
want to go back to rehab or to admit that I had failed, again. Still
groggy from the night before, I looked at the four of them and
knew it was over. I had run out of people to lie to, steal from, and
blame. At dinner, while telling me of the family's decision, my

father started to cry. I had never seen him cry, ever. I agreed to go back into treatment.

Dad had become acquainted with Mitch Rosenthal, the founder of Phoenix House and a man who had contributed greatly to the development of drug therapy and the fight against addiction. Rosenthal had advised my dad to stop enabling me, to cut off all financial and emotional support, which forced me into treatment. The main location of Phoenix House, in the middle of Manhattan, would mean I still had distractions nearby, so we agreed it would be more effective for me to check into the Phoenix House located in Santa Ana, near Los Angeles. I arrived in 1984, and it was very much a sort of military environment, although, for its time, it was a rather progressive treatment facility. Yet it was a harsh environment of behavioral modification therapy. I was stripped of possessions, and I bunked with twenty-five men in an open dormitory, with open shower and toilet stalls. It was culture shock, to say the least. On my second or third day, I was overwhelmed with shame and devastation and began to cry for the first time in years. The dope sickness hadn't even set in yet.

Welcome to your new reality for the next eighteen months, I told myself. Screw it. I'll find a way to get out in a month, two months, tops.

Life Shift

Two months later, I was secretly counting the hours to myself when my father had a sudden heart attack in New York and died at the age of sixty-four. I was devastated. I begged the program director to let me go to his funeral, and I flew home. In between the words of praise at his memorial from Ted Kennedy, Walter Mondale, Mario Cuomo, Christopher Dodd, John Lindsay, and George Steinbrenner, I felt the burden of his shame about me. Although Dad had a long list of accomplishments to his name,

I was simply a sick and lying deviant, and Dad had blamed himself for all of my problems. When we lowered Dad's casket into the ground, I vowed that he would never have to worry about me again.

This moment was a psychic shift for me. I realized how short life is. My father had tried to instill in me honor and dignity and had done the best he could with me. I made a decision to honor his life by living mine in a way that would make him proud. I returned to Phoenix House and was a model resident for eighteen months. I followed the rules, worked in the garden, and opened myself to therapy for the first time. Most important, I developed real relationships. This became the bedrock of my new convictions: in order to stay off drugs, I needed to replace them with human connections. I now wanted what everyone else had: freedom. Oddly enough, for me to achieve freedom, I had to stop doing things "my way." Recovery requires humility. I recall one group session where twenty-five of us residents stayed awake for about fifty hours, sitting on the floor in a circle and talking about our lives. The sleeplessness and the exhaustion ensured that a lot would be uncovered: people talked about murders, rapes, molestations. I talked about my father, about never being good enough, never having his approval. It was very raw and painful. I hope never to endure that pain again.

When my eighteen months came to an end, I was a changed man. I decided that my calling was to work as a counselor for Phoenix House. I returned to New York City and moved into a halfway house on the Upper West Side. I worked with the outpatient adolescent clinic, and I loved it. For the first time in my life, I felt as if I had a purpose.

I wanted to keep changing my life for the better. After a couple years, I decided to move to Los Angeles and start anew. When I got there, I fell crazy into a sort of love addiction with an actress and stumbled in my career path. That was the fallback addiction, Crazy 2.0, which I battled by going to therapy.

It dawned on me that I should go back to school to become a licensed therapist. My lifelong demons began to taunt me about being stupid, but I decided to face my fear, work through my learning disability, and complete graduate school. I was nearly forty, and it took me seven years to get through it (not to mention three tries to pass the licensing exam), but I kicked ass and finally earned my doctorate. I worked as a technician at the Recovery Center in Washington Medical Hospital and then as a counselor at Promises in West Los Angeles, where I worked my way up to program director. During that time, the industry as a whole was reexamining addiction treatment. No longer was it recommended that alcoholics and addicts receive harsh treatment such as boot camps, the type I had endured. Therapists were now in the business of relieving pain, not causing pain. I helped develop state-of-the-art therapy programs for recovering addicts and alcoholics. Today, I own and operate a very attractive facility called the Hills, above Hollywood. Residents have nice rooms and eat great food, but make no mistake: this place is an institution, and it is a battlefield, where we go to war every day. Sometimes the beautiful surroundings are merely one way to seduce an addict into getting help.

We all have that demon inside us. It's the part of our unconscious that tells us we're no good, untalented, and weak. It gets fed by parents who coddle us or spouses who are afraid of us and friends who unwittingly enable us. Our disease is victorious whenever we lie to someone, including ourselves. Your beast wins when you avoid confronting it, especially if you rely on drugs or alcohol to numb the pain and fear. You don't have to be perfect, boring, and holy in order to be happy and sober. You can still be crazy, irreverent, artsy, funny, and offbeat. That's good crazy. My goal is to team up with you to slay that beast and to maintain the parts of you that are unique, offbeat, funny, and charming. Instead of being a villain or a victim, you can fight the disease and emerge the hero, who is still crazy perhaps but clean. Instead of feeling worthless, you can gain control of your own life. I will help you identify your personal demon, and I'll join forces with you to beat the bastard. If anyone knows that enemy, all of its tricks and disguises, how long it can take, and all of the tools you will need to defeat the demon, it is me. Let's go.

2

The Facts behind Alcoholism and Other Addictions

At the Hills Treatment Center in California, we have a program for every addiction, but not all addictions are the same. I discuss the root causes and distinctions in chapters 3 and 4, but it is enlightening to observe just how common the conditions are and to realize that the numbers of addicts are growing. You and I have a lot of company out there, which may offer you some level of consolation. There are also more professionals and support groups available to help you, and we have come a long way in identifying the right treatment for your particular condition, from drinking and drugs to Internet pornography and electronic games.

Most patients I treat are addicted only to alcohol. In fact, 23 percent of all Americans who are in treatment programs are alcoholics. Those who are addicted to other drugs are often addicted to alcohol at the same time—about 18 percent of my patients are addicted to alcohol as well as to something else: pot, cocaine. or heroin. For those who have a propensity for addiction or who are in drug rehab, drinking alcohol provides the "slippery slope" back into full-blown addiction. This is why people recovering from drug addiction need to stay away from alcohol as well, even if drinking is not their main problem.

Obviously, beer, liquor, and wine are easy to obtain, and consuming them is a social ritual for many people, young and old. Our parents drink, our friends drink, our coworkers go out to the bar after work. Many people can drink responsibly and never develop an addiction to alcohol, but others are incapable of controlling their consumption. Millions of people drink alcohol to excess every day, and a lot of alcoholics fuel their disease by "binge" drinking on a regular basis. Binge drinking is when you have five or more drinks on one occasion.

Facts about Binge Drinking
- 57 million Americans over the age of twelve (23 percent of our population) went binge drinking in the last thirty days.
- One in six Americans goes binge drinking every week.
- 28 percent of these American binge drinkers are between ages eighteen and twenty-four.
- 36 percent of those binge drinkers are over age thirty-five.
- Binge drinking is twice as common for men as it is for women, and the rates increase with annual income: 20 percent of those earning $75,000 or more go binge drinking every week.

- For underage drinkers, those ages twelve to twenty, one survey found alcohol use among these groups to be
  - o 18.6 percent among blacks
  - o 19.7 percent among Asians
  - o 25.3 percent among Hispanics
  - o 27.5 percent among those reporting two races
  - o 31.2 percent among American Indians or Alaska Natives
  - o 32.3 percent among whites
- In 2009, more than 30 million Americans reported driving under the influence of alcohol at least once that year.

Marijuana

The next most common addiction is marijuana. This drug is illegal in every state except for California, where it is available legally for residents who have a doctor's prescription. Some states allow the medical use of marijuana (but not its sale), because it can ease the symptoms of cancer, epilepsy, AIDS, and multiple sclerosis. However, I have seen the addiction rate skyrocket in California, because many users manage to obtain prescriptions even when they have no chronic illness.

Pot is one of the most widely distributed illegal narcotics in the world and is certainly the most abused drug. About 17 percent of my patients are addicted to marijuana. It is easy to buy, on the street or at schools, and it's easy to grow. It is the greenish dried flower of the cannabis plant and comes in several varieties, all of which contain tetrahydrocannabinol (THC), which is a mind-altering substance. "Hash" is a compressed preparation of marijuana that usually contains higher levels of THC. It can be smoked in a pipe, rolled with paper into a "joint," and sometimes eaten in baked goods.

Marijuana addicts are getting younger and younger, and the numbers are frightening:

- Nearly 6 percent of twelfth-graders smoke pot on a daily basis.
- 11 percent of all eighth-graders smoked marijuana in 2009.
- Marijuana is by far the most popular illicit drug: 40 percent of all Americans have tried smoking it.
- Marijuana use among teenagers leads to increased rates of lifetime anxiety, depression, and suicidal tendencies.
- Chronic pot smokers are nine times more likely to develop schizophrenia.
- Other health issues related to long-term pot smoking include lung damage, lower fertility, a weakened immune system, and an increased risk of developing certain cancers.
- 9 percent of people who try it become addicted to it.

Although many people are in favor of legalizing marijuana, I have seen firsthand how it can destroy lives. It does alleviate pain and nausea for very sick people, but, for everyone else, it is most certainly a "gateway" to harder drugs, such as cocaine and heroin.

Heroin

In 2009, the average age of a first-time heroin user was twenty-five. One year later, the average age of a first-time heroin user dropped to twenty-one. I have never observed such a rapid growth of narcotics abuse. Roughly 20 percent of our patients at the Hills are addicted to heroin.

- A 2010 study shows that 1.3 percent of American eighth-graders have abused heroin.

- Approximately 20 million people around the world are addicted to heroin.
- A 2009 National Survey on Drug Use and Health reported that 605,000 Americans age twelve and older had used heroin at least once in the previous year.

Heroin is an opiate derived from the morphine in the poppy flower, which is often grown in Mexico and Afghanistan. It has been used for decades as a pain reliever for surgery and other physical trauma, but recreational users like it for its ability to induce relaxation and euphoria. Frequent users need to take more and more heroin to feel the effects and, before long, they might be spending six hundred dollars a day on their habit. In addition to dependence on the drug, users often contract hepatitis and HIV from using dirty needles. Heroin has little effect if it is swallowed as a pill, so users who seek the rush will inject it, which is also known as "mainlining" and "shooting up." The powder is mixed with water and injected with a hypodermic needle into the arm or less obvious places, such as the legs or the feet. The powder can also be snorted like cocaine or smoked by vaporizing it in a glass pipe. Heroin users are susceptible not only to addiction, but also to accidental overdose. This is what killed Jerry Garcia, Jimi Hendrix, and Jim Morrison and contributed to the deaths of Kurt Cobain and Amy Winehouse.

Cocaine

Cocaine is an alkaloid derived from the coca plant and is famous for once having been a vital ingredient in the original formula for a certain cola drink. This powerful stimulant is usually snorted in powder form, but it is also smoked in a pipe, which crackles when the powder vaporizes, hence the street name, "crack" cocaine. It makes the user feel more alert, euphoric, and energetic, and its effects last for roughly twenty minutes before the user wants to have more. About 10 percent of the patients at the Hills have a cocaine addiction in one form or another.

Using this drug decreases your brain's natural levels of serotonin and dopamine, which makes coming down from it particularly difficult and addiction very hard to kick. Regular users also have twice the normal risk of having a stroke or a heart attack. Sometimes cocaine is combined with heroin in a syringe as a "speedball." Over time, abusers build up a tolerance and need to use more of the drug, more frequently. Cocaine addicts feel intense cravings for months, even years, after quitting. As such, they frequently turn to alcohol or other drugs to help curb the desire for coke.

- The United States is the leading global consumer of cocaine.
- 40 million Americans ages twelve and over have tried cocaine at least once.
- 25 percent of Americans between the ages of twenty-six and thirty-four have tried cocaine.
- 6 percent of those who try cocaine become addicts.
- Teens who drink alcohol are *50 times* more likely to try cocaine.
- 40 percent of all high school students have used cocaine.

Methamphetamine

Methamphetamine—"crystal meth," "crystal," "ice," "tina," "T," or "crank"—is a prescription drug that doctors might provide to patients for treatment of depression or Parkinson's disease. It induces euphoria, energy, and even an increased sex drive. In recent years, users have concocted their own recipes in illegal "meth labs," and business is booming. Much cheaper than cocaine, meth has soared in popularity and is highly addictive.

Users might stay awake for days. Many addicts—up to 25 percent of them—develop psychoses similar to schizophrenia, which take months to go away. Meth is injected, snorted, and smoked, and chronic users have teeth that rot and often fall out, hence "meth mouth." About 7 percent of patients at the Hills are addicted to meth, but that number gets larger every year.

- In 2009 alone, 1.2 million Americans ages twelve and over had abused methamphetamines.
- Methamphetamines can be taken orally, injected with a syringe, snorted, or smoked.
- Volatile chemical reactions cause explosions in home-based "meth labs," which have killed scores of people in recent years.
- Meth is infamous for being addictive for ninety-eight percent of the people who try it, even just once. Studies will show it is somewhat less than that figure, no doubt. However, a recent study of several large California communities showed that fifty percent of the people arrested had meth in their systems.
- Women are more likely to get addicted to meth than they are to cocaine.

What Are Bath Salts?

Numerous news stories have reported on psychotic reactions to synthetic drug compounds known colloquially as "bath salts," which usually contain mephedrone or methylone and sidestep federal laws by calling themselves bath salts "not for human consumption." These are variations of designer street drugs that cause psychosis, hallucinations, paranoia, and suicide. I can't say any of these are necessarily addictive, because their ingredients are constantly changing, but they are certainly dangerous, and federal laws are being created to control their production and distribution.

Painkillers

People also get addicted to opiates other than heroin, in the form of painkillers, such as Vicodin, Demerol, and OxyContin, among other varieties of prescription pills. About 10 percent of our patients are addicted to painkillers. Although these drugs are important for people who suffer from chronic pain, they might be illicitly used by individuals who consume them merely to get high, or because they became addicted after taking a legitimate prescription for an injury. Teenagers love to find such pills in their parents' medicine cabinets, if for no other reason than to experiment with them. Although teens were once able to crush Oxy pills and snort them like cocaine to get a powerful rush, the manufacturer has gotten wise: the OxyContin brand is now in a gel capsule form that is impossible to crush into a powder.

Addiction treatment for painkillers uses a multifaceted approach, beginning with detox, which is very important because withdrawal symptoms from these drugs are painful and powerful.

- Vicodin (hydrocodone) and OxyContin (oxycodone) are partly synthetic opiates marketed by pharmaceutical companies to treat physical pain. Currently, they are the most commonly abused of all prescription narcotics. They most often appear in the form of a tablet, in which the hydrocodone or oxycodone is mixed with acetaminophen or aspirin.
- 50 percent of all users of painkillers are doing so without a prescription.

- These narcotic prescriptions have the same addiction rate as heroin.
- Use of these drugs by U.S. high school students increases 1 percent per year; the drugs are largely obtained from their parents—patients with prescriptions whose children steal from the medicine bottles.
- 1.2 million patients visited the emergency room in 2009 after abusing painkillers, an increase of 100 percent in five years.
- The number of people seeking treatment for addiction to painkillers has increased 400 percent in the last decade.

Stimulants

The most common stimulants are prescription drugs that were developed for attention deficit disorder, such as Ritalin and Adderall. They are now abused regularly, often by high school or college students who want to focus on their studies.

- Ritalin abuse is on the rise among high-schoolers, largely due to the availability of the drug in prescription form. A University of Michigan study reveals that more high-schoolers use Ritalin (aka methylphenidate) than do those who have legitimate prescriptions for it.
- More than 10 percent of ninth-graders reported the illicit use of Ritalin at least once.
- Many take Ritalin or Adderall to stay awake (either for studying or for binge drinking) or to lose weight.
- A 2011 study revealed that 25 percent of college students use Adderall (amphetamines) as a study aid.
- Ritalin and Adderall are highly addictive—some studies suggest that more than 50 percent of people who try them become addicted.

Depressants

People who suffer from anxiety or panic attacks or who have trouble sleeping frequently become addicted to drugs such as benzodiazepines, "central nervous system" drugs such as Valium, Xanax, Ativan, and Klonopin. I almost always see this kind of addiction coexist with addictions to stimulants or opiates, because these "downers" are used to counter the effects of, and come down from, the other drugs.

Behavioral Addictions

Compulsive repetitive behavior that is not related to drugs or alcohol can still be damaging to yourself and others. Gambling, overeating, and risky sex are among certain behaviors that are affected by brain chemicals, and which sometimes require a recovery program to help you regain control of these behaviors. We are seeing more and more young people who are addicted to texting on their smartphones, to the extent that they are causing fatal car accidents, and I anticipate that we will be treating more and more behavioral addictions in the years to come. Here are the more common behavioral addictions we currently treat in our recovery facility:

Love Addiction

After I got sober, I became addicted to what I thought was love. It wasn't about sex necessarily (see below), but about falling in love repeatedly, to the point of worship, and usually with someone who was not as reciprocal. Perhaps I got this tendency from my mother, who wanted nothing from the world except my father's undivided love. The emotional highs and lows can lead to compulsive and self-destructive behavior. I worked through this addiction with counseling, and learned how to develop healthy relationships that eventually led to the love of my life.

Sex Addiction

- Sex addiction is an intimacy disorder characterized by compulsive sexual thoughts and escalating sexual behavior, which progresses until it has a negative impact on the addict and the whole family.
- Sex addicts seek out multiple partners or obsess about unattainable partners.
- Between 3 percent and 5 percent of Americans suffer from this disorder, which is often associated with depression.
- Pornography addiction falls under this category as well.
- Treatment is similar to other treatments for addiction, including therapy and 12-step programs. However, the goal is not lifelong abstinence, but ending the unhealthy behavior. In order for addicts to learn the difference between healthy and unhealthy sex, many programs recommend abstinence for the first ninety days of treatment.

Pornography Addiction

- People who are addicted to pornography use this "drug of choice" to replace important relationships and commitments. They isolate themselves for hours each day, unable to stop, trying to keep their addiction a secret.
- Porn addicts use their computers or cell phones to watch porn movies or even to meet anonymous sex partners.
- 25 million Americans visit cybersex websites between one and ten hours per week. Nearly 5 million spend more than eleven hours a week on these sites.
- Psychotherapy and 12-step groups such as Sex Addicts Anonymous can treat this addiction, which is usually a less painful process than recovering from drugs or alcohol abuse.

Video Game Addiction

- Some psychology associations estimate that nearly 9 percent of American young people are addicted to playing video games, particularly role-playing games. Children who play games for four or five hours a day then leave no time for socializing, sports, or homework.

- This addiction is defined as impulse control that is damaging to other functioning, and it is believed to be related to the release of dopamine.

- Game addicts exhibit the same traits as alcoholics—they need to do it more and more, and they are angry or miserable if they must stop.

- Game addiction takes away from normal social development, an effect that can last a lifetime.

- Detox programs retrain abusers to use computers without playing games. Kids learn that real-life excitement can take the place of their addiction.

Gambling Addiction

- Compulsive behaviors often include betting on sports, playing the lottery, attending poker games, and playing slot machines.

- Between 2 percent and 5 percent of Americans have this addiction, and most of them actually suffer from a coexisting disorder, such as alcoholism or a personality disorder.

- 75 percent of these addicts are men, although the proportion of women is on the rise.

- Treatment includes psychotherapy and Gamblers Anonymous meetings.

- Certain antiseizure medications (such as Topamax) seem to reduce the "thrill" associated with gambling. Other patients also do well with antidepressants or medications for the coexisting psychological condition.
- Some medications for Parkinson's disease and multiple sclerosis actually cause a compulsion for gambling.

Believe It or Not, the Recovery Processes Are Virtually the Same

Whether your issues are with drugs and alcohol or with compulsive behaviors, the healing processes are very similar. It's all about getting effective counseling and training the brain to respond differently to familiar triggers. A compulsive gambler does not necessarily have the same challenges as a heroin addict, but we have learned that the most successful recovery programs contain the same core elements. We tailor certain aspects to fit the problem, but, by and large, the Hills program is very effective for any type of addiction.

3

Dealing with the Demon

Many of us who are addicts or alcoholics are, in large part, enslaved to a part of our personalities that some people, including me, refer to as a "beast." This is our demonic side, as opposed to our happy, healthy, creative nature that makes up our authentic self. Of course, in many instances, our addictions are also physiological; I describe the role of our brain chemistry in the next chapter. Yet my program focuses specifically on identifying and confronting this damaging psychological element inside us, because I have learned that this can be the greatest challenge to recovery.

This volatile creature lives inside of everyone, whether you're an addict or not. It's the part of you that indulges in "acting out": cheating on your wife, slugging someone, overeating in the middle of the night, spending $5,000 on a purse, gambling away your children's college fund, using heroin. This is the part of you that needs instant gratification, the part of you that is not comfortable in your own skin and needs something "outside" of yourself to make you feel better. It is the part of you that says you don't deserve to be happy.

My demon was the one who told me, "You're stupid." My father went to MIT, my brother went to MIT and Harvard Law, my sisters went to Columbia and Sarah Lawrence, and I had a horrible learning disability. Buried deep inside me, my beast was constantly telling me how stupid I was. It manifested and grew louder whenever I brought home a lousy report card, whenever I transgressed to the point of getting myself kicked out of a school. I felt somewhat better only when I got high, which numbed the beast that always knocked me down.

My Own Best Negative Reinforcement

You may hear a voice in your head that always tells you you're overweight, or that you'll never write a good novel or be as successful as your father. Those internal demons might be confirming things you hear from your verbally abusive boss or from your mother (who has always accused you of making bad decisions).

* * *

I have a client named Jeri, whose husband is simply never home. She has a lovely home and several good friends, and has learned how to garden to compensate for her time alone. Mike travels for work, and Jeri learned that he has had several affairs with coworkers, to which he confessed but continues to pursue. Jeri has sought counseling with me (for which Mike has "no time") and is learning that this marital situation is not sustainable. Her demon is a lack of self-esteem (propped up by her husband's emotional abuse), and she is uncertain whether she deserves to stand up for herself. We're still working on these issues with Jeri and her "demon" of self-doubt.

•   •   •

Lousy relationships are a good example of your disease being in control of your life. Men and women often pick unavailable or the worst possible partners. Many psychotherapists attribute this to their trying to meet unmet needs from childhood. Many people have "pickers" that are broken. This is your beast at work.

Many of my clients are young men in their teens and twenties from affluent families. Their parents are successful and are often busy at work. Similar to me as a teenager, they live in luxurious homes, drive hot cars, and are largely left to their own devices on a daily basis. Money is no object to these kids, so they get their kicks by acting as daring as they can; that almost always includes drinking and drugs. I had a patient named Patrick who was one of these guys: the life of the party at his college fraternity and a huge sports fan, yet he secretly drank about half a gallon of vodka every day. He got kicked out of school and even went to rehab once or twice before I met him. When he came to our first appointment, I could tell that he was still drinking, although he denied it. I was heartened by the fact that he was in my office, in any event, so we kept meeting on a weekly basis. We'd talk about football, and he thought he had me fooled. He acted compliant and sober, but I had been in his shoes, so I recognized the manipulation. I didn't call him on it, though. I knew that when he was ready, he would do that himself. Nearly twelve months later, after establishing a nice relationship of trust, he broke down with me. It had taken a while, but his psychic shift finally took hold. Patrick has been sober now for four years. I think he's in a great place.

Obsessive Thinking

Your destructive persona is often reinforced by endless cycles of obsessive thinking. We all have that "monkey mind"—the constant chatter in our heads that is sometimes hard to turn off when we want to focus our attention or simply fall asleep. When your disease is in charge, those thoughts turn more and more to the negative. My colleague Nick Mouyiaris, a recovered addict who is now a therapist at the Hills, surveys his patients to illustrate this tendency. When he asks someone to write down all of her thoughts inside a sixty-second period, she might write down ten or twenty different thoughts. That means she has a couple hundred thoughts every hour, and she most likely repeats the thoughts that are negative. This is why something as minor as getting a parking ticket can ruin your entire day. This is the work of your inner demon.

Sigmund Freud called this part of ourselves the "Id":

It is the dark, inaccessible part of our personality, what little we know of it we have learned from our study of the dream-work and of the construction of neurotic symptoms, and most of that is of a negative character and can be described only as a contrast to the ego. We approach the id with analogies: we call it a chaos, a cauldron full of seething excitations.... It is filled with energy reaching it from the instincts, but it has no organization, produces no collective will, but only a striving to bring about the satisfaction of the instinctual needs subject to the observance of the pleasure principle.

Others might call it our "shadow," the part of us that holds forbidden feelings such as rage, lust and shame. And they can be exacerbated by trauma—such as assault—and also by too much self-medication with alcohol or drugs. Karl Jung described the shadow as instinctive and irrational, and that it tended to project itself onto others: one's own personal inferiority often becomes a "moral deficiency" in someone else.

We can't control the fact that this part exists inside each of us. Most of the time, it seems, we are oblivious to our demon's existence and its causes, or we instinctively cope with it in harmless ways. If you are aware of it, though, you can choose how to cope with it. Some people plant themselves in front of a TV set or a computer all day, which is another way to avoid real life. Others get therapy, recognize their issues, and learn to enjoy life in spite of these beasts. Many people deal with it by drinking or using drugs.

The Genetic Curse

Alcoholism and addiction are defined as chronic and progressive diseases with genetic, psychosocial, and environmental factors. Experts say that 40 percent of a predisposition is due to genetic factors, although there is no single addiction gene. The body becomes dependent on alcohol or drugs, and the individual loses control over the amount and frequency of his consumption. If one of your parents has a problem with drinking or drugs, you are three or four times more likely to develop the problem yourself, in some way or another. For example, 75 percent of cocaine addicts have at least one parent who is an alcoholic. Your brain is probably already wired with different "reward nerves" and develops higher thresholds for pleasure than the average person's brain. Yet genetics is not the only factor.

We know addiction is not a failure of willpower or an unwillingness to take responsibility or a moral failing. The effects of this disease have nothing to do with your family income, religion, race, education, neighborhood, or age. It is more prevalent in people who have a family history of addiction and tends to occur simply from regular exposure to alcohol or drugs over time. It is also more common if you suffer from depression or other mental health problems. The symptoms are these: the inability to control the frequency and amount of drinking or drugging, even after your behavior has a negative impact on your life, such as a failed marriage, legal problems, or losing your job. You build up tolerance for increasing amounts of alcohol or drugs, you start placing great importance on when or where you will use—to the exclusion of caring about family, friends, or work—and you may suffer physical or psychological pain if you stop consuming them. Addicts appear to want pleasure more, but they actually enjoy it less. So they must consume more alcohol or drugs, yet they achieve less pleasure from them. You know you need professional help if you are drinking or using drugs to excess, if you have caused physical injury to yourself or someone else or have lost a job, if you have lost control of when and how much you consume, and if alcohol or drugs have become necessary for you to perform even normal functions.

Behavioral addiction may include cigarette smoking, having sex, playing video games, surfing the Internet, or gambling. Many people don't consider these real addictions, but they certainly are. People addicted to these behaviors can do things just as crazy as an alcoholic or a drug user.

* * *

I have a patient named Rick who is very smart. He got addicted to video games in college, perhaps because he was intimidated by other students there who were also very smart. He played *Modern Warfare* for hours every day, stopped going to classes, and dropped out of school. He thought he could kick his habit, all on his own. Yet now he simply played the game in secret, telling others that he was still in school, and borrowing money on student loans. He fell deeply in debt and grew ashamed.

I have a patient, Melanie, who is a hard-core heroin addict at the age of twenty-five. She was abused as a child, one of the most common yet unrecognized sources of shame and guilt. Her mother's boyfriend had molested her, beginning at age ten, for about four years. From a very young age, drinking and drugging were easy options for her when she wanted to bury the pain and the confusion. After ten years as an addict, she simply doesn't know how to live a normal life.

Another patient, Dan, has gambled away every dime he ever had—as well as some that belonged to his wife, his parents, and his brother. He didn't lose money at the poker table: he lost it chasing one bad business "investment idea" after another. His wife eventually left him, he lost his job, and he abandoned his house and mortgage. He is forty years old now, drinking heavily, and blaming his financial losses and misfortunes on a long list of other people. Addiction is still in charge of Dan.

* * *

Regardless of genetics or brain chemistry, it is certain that most users and drinkers do so to "self-medicate": we are numbing ourselves from whatever psychological trauma or condition has manifested in that beast.

It's one thing to try a drug to get high and not use it again. It is another thing to use it more and more often, almost always in an attempt to feel better about oneself. If you are depressed or have attention deficit disorder, for example, cocaine is a terrific antidote. If your particular type of crazy is depression or attention deficit disorder, coke is—let's face it—an effective remedy. It lifts your spirits, gives you energy, and improves your ability to focus.

Its effects are instantaneous, similar to all drugs, and we are by nature rather impatient creatures who love instant gratification. Yet coming off coke creates an even deeper depression, and using more and more drugs creates a more intense need for the drug and removes any other natural talent you may have for coping with depression or attention deficit disorder.

Other addicts are simple thrill-seekers who are always pushing the edge to feel an adrenaline rush. Some of these people do daring things and "try" drugs without becoming addicts. They can put a crack pipe down and never do it again. But for those who use drugs or alcohol more and more often, the aim is not so much to get high, but to alleviate pain or depression or even to avoid withdrawal itself. Often, the comedown is so bad that someone will use again merely to offset the "hangover." These people aren't getting loaded to enhance their lives. They're caught in a dreadful cycle of addiction.

There is a "pleasure pathway" in the brain that lights up when we experience pleasure. Some people feel it while having sex or playing video games, shopping, eating chocolate, or drinking a scotch. In moderation, there's nothing wrong with this, but when we do anything too much, the brain starts to withhold our pleasure receptors, and we want to do it more and more frequently to regain that high. Then we *need* to do it more. If we go without it, we become restless, anxious, depressed, and irritable. The addiction has taken hold, and we start obsessing, even when it has a negative impact on us. Our pleasure pathway has been overused, and we are now oversensitive to it: we feel a trigger every time we turn on the computer or see someone else drinking a beer. Cravings can override normal brain function, but we can't resist the urge, and, in the end, we succumb and feel guilt and shame. Certainly, some addictions, such as gambling or shopping, may have less lethal effects than drinking and doing drugs, but the compulsion is the same, and the driving force behind it is the same—your disease.

The Defense Mechanism

The desire to soothe your anxiety and the ability to calm yourself without assistance are talents developed between the ages of one and three. Toddlers seem to learn how to do this from mimicking the attitudes of their parents. Attention and encouragement at this stage of childhood are vital; without this parental support—if the parents are distant or absent—the child is bereft of how to handle anxiety and stress on his own. This is evident with compulsive eaters, for example, who have long used food as a comfort in the absence of parental attention.

"Addicts tend to believe that they are not the masters of their own fate, that control lies outside of them," says Robert B. Millman, an addiction expert at New York Hospital-Cornell Medical School.

The Egotistical Monster

In addition to poor coping skills, some addicts are simply narcissists who think "no one understands them," It is a myth that creative people are more likely to be addicts. Amy Winehouse, Michael Jackson, Chris Farley, Jimi Hendrix, and John Belushi were great artists, but they were done in by the same old demon that you and I cope with every day. In their case, they were working in a business that is rife with drink and drugs. While they may have struggled to remain at the top of their creative form, they also fought against the addiction craziness that ultimately took their lives.

Two personality traits seem to indicate a predisposition toward addiction: risk-taking and shyness. Studies confirm that young people who are shy or who like to be daring are more likely to develop an unhealthy addiction later in life. Everyone has unique circumstances that set him or her up for addictive behavior, however, and my experience has shown me that this "bad crazy" grows from a wide variety of issues. It's a combination of genetics, personality, and peer pressure, but also preexisting emotions such as anxiety, loneliness, or depression. Major stress or trauma can contribute to a drug dependency as well. Our defense mechanisms against these feelings might be denial, rationalization, or projection, or we might resort to gambling, drinking, smoking pot, or shooting heroin.

We need to learn how to cope with the disease and also with the triggers that enable it to regain control over us. One way we do that is by learning how to communicate exactly what we think and feel. Part of that is learned from therapists, but we also learn from other addicts.

"Addicts sort life through their differences to other people, not their similarities," says my colleague Jorja Davis, a counselor at the Hills. "We need to be taught to look at the similarities between us and other people."

The Austrian psychologist Viktor Frankl wrote, "When we are no longer able to change a situation, we are challenged to change ourselves."

When you can express yourself in words, it allows you to let the feelings go. At the same time, this expression starts to diminish the stranglehold of your beast. This act of talking or writing in a journal almost becomes something spiritual, because you're no longer disconnected from the rest of the world. Expressing your true feelings and thoughts can make you feel at peace. It's not easy people stay in bad relationships or drink and do drugs in order to avoid the pain of thinking or talking about difficult things.

Learning how to express yourself can feel even more liberating than getting high. Reaching your inner self frees you from ego and fear. Our disease gives us arrogance, which we hide behind when we are weak and are afraid we'll be discovered as such. Yet if you deny that you have a problem and believe you "have all the answers," you can't learn anything. If you can't learn anything, then you won't get better. Reaching your inner self also allows you to accept responsibility for who you are and what you've done, rather than blaming others and playing the victim. It is so easy to blame others for your shortcomings. All addicts do it. I blamed my dad, my mom, Richard Nixon, the war machine. I blamed everybody. I said, "Fuck you!" to all of them, but I was really saying, "Fuck you!" to myself. I was the only one taking drugs. I took my anger and shot it up my arm. I knew what I was doing. I knew I was destroying myself, but I didn't care. I wasn't suicidal; I just didn't care. I was crazy, in a bad way.

It's not so terrible to accept responsibility for your own actions. It is, by definition, empowering. In addition to learning how to communicate effectively, you can take a major step toward sobriety by avoiding the triggers. I'm not just talking about staying away from booze and coke. I mean avoiding the apartment, the neighborhood, the nightclubs, the dorm, the party friends, the cruising, the seductress with a habit, the sexy guy with a line, the reggae concert, or the sports bar—any of these could act as a trigger and cause you to backslide.

One of the most profound influences on addiction and recovery is social pressure. We all want to have relationships with our peers, and no one is more influenced by that desire than a teenager. Kids might start to drink and use drugs to be cool with their friends, but they are still developing and are therefore the most vulnerable to addiction. It's so easy for them to get access to drugs and alcohol. Dealers are everywhere now: not just in dicey neighborhoods but at your local shopping mall, suburban fast-food restaurant, and ritzy private school.

You or your family member will not emerge from these cycles without professional help. I encourage you to find a therapist or a program and meet there at least twice a week and as often as seven days a week. I am sharing my patients' stories with you to show you the role I play—and that your own therapist should play—in this whole process. My goal is to create an alliance with you that will fight against your demon. The team will be you—your good crazy—and me, against your disease. You and your therapist, against that evil entity inside you. Two against one. The problem is, many addicts don't want to be part of their own team. If you don't take part, then the therapist can't form an alliance with you. You must also join in the fight.

The Wall Is Not a Door

Many addicts (and their families) remain in denial for quite a while—and many of these patients are still using drugs or drinking. I tell a patient that starting on the road to recovery is as easy as opening a door and walking through it. I stand up, walk to the door, and say, "Follow me!" There's no resistance when you turn the handle and walk through. With many patients, though, it is as if they prefer to believe that the wall is a door. They think they are able to drink, and it won't lead to snorting cocaine again. They don't walk through the door to recovery; they believe the wall is the door. They're hitting their head against the wall, telling me it is a door.

Let's face it, it's crazy to believe that a wall is a door. I have to convince many a patient to follow me to an actual door. Walking through it is easy, and life can be great. Follow me; there is no resistance to walking through it.

These stubborn patients eventually call me in the middle of the night, bombed out of their skulls, and ask for help. I don't say,

"I told you so." It's not a matter of who's right and who's wrong. Every time a patient tries again and comes back to me, he or she is a little more willing.

The process of acknowledging your problem and getting sober can be a drag. You will need patience, but it's time for you to take part in your own life. You're not a victim of outside circumstances. It is up to you. It's never too late to finally start on the road to happiness.

4

The Role of the Brain in Addiction

The primary reason anyone drinks or takes drugs is to feel better. We want to give ourselves a reward to make up for something that has injured us in some way. We take a painkiller, a line of coke, or a hit of weed, and we start to feel good pretty quickly. We like it so much, we do some more. Then we have to do even more to feel the good effects. This is physically changing the pathways inside our brains.

The basis for all addiction is the neurochemical dopamine. The brain releases dopamine in response to activities such as eating, exercising, having sex, taking risks, and using drugs. Dopamine facilitates our ability to experience pleasure, and we get a "high" feeling. When we fall in love, we are high on these neurochemicals. Because it feels so good, we tend to repeat the actions that cause the release of dopamine. Amphetamines, opiates, cocaine, and methamphetamines overload the brain with dopamine, bringing a sense of euphoria. It is human nature to want more.

Alcohol and certain drugs such as LSD affect the release of serotonin, another neurotransmitter chemical. As with dopamine, when serotonin levels are altered by our using drugs, the brain is fooled into thinking that "normal" status is when it's loaded with drugs. So the brain releases fewer of these chemicals naturally, causing a physical imbalance that drives a person to try to get more serotonin in the bloodstream, by using drugs and alcohol.

Some people are simply born with fewer receptors for these pleasure chemicals, which causes a similar dysfunction in the brain at an early age. Studies identify this condition in certain toddlers who crave things before they even fully understand what those things are. These children often show little confidence in themselves, which lasts their entire lives. We cannot change the cell structure we were born with. Parents would do their children a world of favors by encouraging them and guiding them in their early decisions, long before they even start first grade.

Other conditions inside the brain can also influence your susceptibility to drug addiction and alcoholism.

Frontal Lobe Development

Many parents have observed that their children change seemingly overnight. Sometimes it happens literally: your sweet son suddenly dyes his hair black and pierces his eyebrow. Your daughter goes from straight A's to skipping classes and then has a car accident. Thanks to technologies such as magnetic resonance imaging (MRI), scientists can now see the stages of the teenage brain in development. It is clear that the frontal lobe of the brain is undergoing a sea change during the teen years, a process that continues until well into our twenties.

In addition to the chemical balance and the release of dopamine playing a role in the propensity for addiction, so does the development of the frontal lobes of our brains. This is where the brain carries out "executive" functions—planning, goal-setting, insight, and judgment—and it is believed that the frontal lobe influences our emotional reactions. Because of this, teenagers do not have speedy "adult" thought processes about actions and their consequences. In other words, their judgment is impaired even when they are totally sober.

New studies have revealed that the brain undergoes total reorganization and rewiring between the ages of twelve and twenty-five. Neurotransmitters and receptors grow a hundredfold during this period, and synapses that are not used much start to shrink. The changes start at the back of the brain—where memories are stored—and slowly move to the frontal lobe, where we make decisions. Brains get better at balancing impulses, goals, and ethics, thus generating behavior that is more complex and more sensible. Yet this takes years of finesse—in teenagers, the process is still clumsy and unreliable. Although they may be supersensitive to emotions, teens are often not yet able to identify those emotions. This means that, overall, the teenage brain is far more sensitive than at any other stage of human life. The teen years are a window in time when the brain is most susceptible to experiences.

The development in the frontal lobe can also be affected by head trauma, such as a concussion, at any time during infancy and childhood. Lifetime damage can occur from shaking a baby, a football injury, or even emotional trauma. Children who suffer psychological abuse or neglect thus learn to live in a hyperalert state, negotiating emotional chaos in a constant survival mode, which will permanently alter the brain's use of serotonin. This or any injury to the frontal lobe can affect a person's brain and thought processes for the rest of her life.

Teens Have It Tough

In teenagers, stress, fatigue, and environment can easily cause the brain to further malfunction. Due to its sensitivity, the teen's brain is slower at "reading" other people, including his or her parents. The teenager's changing brain misinterprets a parent's attitude as angry or sad, even when it's not, and then reacts inappropriately. Miscommunication abounds.

Most teens can reason as well as adults can, but they weigh risk very differently than adults do. Teens greatly value the rewards of the risk—and this reward is frequently the attention of other people, specifically, people their own age. Many risks are necessary for success in life—moving away from one's parents, for example, and starting a job are new adventures, after all. Teens must learn to be adaptive and resilient, but it takes a few years to develop sound judgment. At the same time that these changes are occurring in the brain, the average teenager is adapting to adulthood and preparing to go out on his own. We know that teens love new things, which also means taking risks—driving fast (while texting!), skydiving—and this is the same trait that offers positive developments. For example, it also encourages teens to make new friends, which is important for a lifetime of positive social structure.

Teens invest their time with other teens because they offer more novelty than family members do and also because building relationships with peers is an investment in their future. According to David Dobbs in *National Geographic* magazine, we humans are highly social creatures—teens perceive social exclusion as a threat to their very existence. That's why teens can get hysterical about the ups and downs of their social lives. Similar traits are found in all human cultures, modern or not; it is not just an American syndrome. Teens everywhere seek novelty, excitement, and new peers.

* * *

I have a seventeen-year-old patient named Marlis who thought she could beat her addiction to heroin by using marijuana instead. I once thought the same thing about my cocaine addiction. In no time, Marlis went from smoking pot to becoming addicted to pot, which set her on the path to resuming heroin within a couple of months. When you are an addict, you will get addicted to other drugs and alcohol, and they will quickly send you down the spiral back to the bottom.

Daniel, fifteen, was painfully shy at school, although he had one or two outcast-type friends. He had started drinking bourbon with them, to escape the stress, at the age of thirteen. He stole liquor from his parents' house and was caught twice, but they attributed it to normal behavior. When Daniel was arrested during a drunken fight at a fast-food restaurant, his parents came to me. He has been sober now for just one month. Because he is still so young, we are implementing a plan where Daniel sees a counselor every day, and three times a week he joins a group of former addicts who are the same age as him. He is still living with his parents (who discarded all of the alcohol in the house) but is essentially in a sober living environment. We are hopeful that we can transform his early tendency to addiction into a healthier adulthood, by intervening before he has caused too much damage to his adolescent brain.

* * *

Extreme shyness and great risk taking are predictors of addictive behavior. It is easier to guide young people with these traits before they are exposed to drinking and drugs. Studies show that parents who talk to their kids about drugs and alcohol can help prevent their kids' subsequent use of, and addiction to, these substances. All parents need to lend a steady hand during adolescence, by staying connected but allowing independence, and trying to share information with the voice of experience, rather than one of authority. Teens prefer to follow their peers for guidance, but during this period, the brain is being hard-wired, and we must remember how sensitive their brains are to everything around them. They do not take in information and process it the same way adults do. Therefore, every dinner table conversation, every text message or phone call may be understood very differently by a parent and a teenager.

The brain goes through this volatile metamorphosis whether or not your child is drinking or using drugs. Yet knowing how the dopamine and serotonin levels can be altered by substances during this crucial stage of brain development, we begin to understand how confronting addiction in a young person can seem like an impenetrable problem. If addiction is untreated for many years, the chemical balance and the frontal lobes are probably beyond repair. We cannot change the cells in our bodies, but we can manage them, much the same way that we do with people who are clinically depressed. This means using not only prescription medications to alleviate the gaps in brain function, but also psychotherapy. As I learned from my practice and from scientific studies, achieving peace and self-fulfillment and working with others can actually increase the blood flow to the frontal lobe. My program in this book encompasses steps that can bring this remedial effect to you. My colleague Jorja Davis reminds patients that they will learn to distinguish themselves and regain control of their lives, instead of letting the brain's desire for drugs drive their behavior. Sometimes simply understanding the role of the brain helps you separate the nature of desire from your behavior and free will.

Not all addicts have frontal lobes that are impaired, and many of my patients are well beyond those teen years when the brain is most vulnerable. Yet a good number of patients do suffer from clinical depression. Not all people with depression are alcoholics or addicts, but many of those with a substance abuse problem are self-medicating because they suffer from depression that is undiagnosed.

Depression

A study by the National Institute of Mental Health determined that one-third of people who have depression will also abuse drugs or alcohol. Some experts believe that women will develop depression and then start self-medicating with alcohol and pills. Men are more likely to start overdrinking and using drugs, and they develop depression as a result of their addiction. Alcoholics of either gender are three to four times more likely to have depression.

Former U.S. senator George McGovern wrote a painfully moving account of his daughter's struggle with depression and alcoholism. In his book, *Terry* (1997), he wrote, "Terry was dealt a double cruel hand: the companion demons depression and alcoholism. They were demons that warred ceaselessly against the other aspects of her being—a warm and sunny disposition." Terry had died after passing out drunk in the snow and freezing to death.

Many patients with these dual demons also suffer from bipolar disorder, mood or anxiety disorders, schizophrenia, or suicidal tendencies, some of which are genetically inherited. Studies show that stopping the addiction does improve the symptoms of depression. Certainly, the depression will not be cured if the patient is still abusing drugs or alcohol. Alcohol in itself is a depressant. If you are taking an antidepressant and still drinking heavily, then your antidepressant medication is not working!

Treatments for depression include counseling and behavioral therapy, antidepressant medications, and, for the most severe cases, electroconvulsive therapy (ECT). As with addiction, success in treating depression relies on the engagement of the patient in his or her own recovery. And, as with addiction, it is most beneficial if the entire family enters counseling together, because these dual conditions do a real number on the family as a whole.

Anxiety

Fifteen million Americans suffer from anxiety disorder—low self-esteem, phobias, and panic attacks—and as many as 15 percent of those people are addicted to illicit drugs such as marijuana and cocaine. Alcohol and drugs help such people "relax," often to the point where the addiction becomes more problematic than the original anxiety condition. Anxiety is successfully treated with psychotherapy and sometimes with prescription medication, and a number of support networks can be found in communities and on the Internet for people who suffer from this disorder.

Treating depression or anxiety is not a cure for addiction, however. The only way to get sober is to confront your fears through psychotherapy or counseling and working the 12 steps. There is no magic pill for addiction. After I was sober for twenty-three years, I started taking an antidepressant. Taking Lexapro has enhanced my sobriety—I observe that I am less obsessive in my thinking. In the past, I often became anxious about something and created a crisis when there was none. Now that I'm taking this antidepressant, I am able to easily solve a problem without turning to negative thoughts. I can "turn the channel" more quickly without rehashing the past. It turns out that obsessive thinking runs in my family: my mother and several siblings have the same issue. Yet medication alone would never have gotten me sober.

Here are some of the most common and effective antidepressants used by some of my patients:

Selective Serotonin Reuptake Inhibitors (SSRIs)
Celexa (citalopram)
Lexapro (escitalopram oxalate)
Luvox (paroxetine)
Prozac (fluoxetine)
Zoloft (sertraline)

Serotonin-Norepinephrine Reuptake Inhibitors (SNRIs)
Cymbalta (duloxetine)
Effexor (venlafaxine)
Pristiq (desvenlafaxine)

Monoamine Oxidase Inhibitors (MAOIs)
Nardil (phenelzine)
Parnate (tranylcypromine)

Tricyclic Antidepressants (TCAs)
Adapin (doxepin)
Anafranil (clomipramine)
Elavil or Endep (amitriptyline)
Ludiomil (maprotiline)
Norpramin or Pertofrane (desipramine)
Pamelor (nortryptyline)
Sinequan (doxepin)
Surmontil (trimipramine)
Tofranil (imipramine)
Vivactil (protriptyline)

Other Antidepressants
Buspar (buspirone)
Desyrel (trazodone)
Edronax or Vestra (reboxetine)
Remeron (mirtazapine)
Serzone (nefazodone)
Wellbutrin (bupropion)

Psychologists and rehabilitation counselors know how to treat addicts who also suffer from depression or other disorders. Successfully treating the symptoms of depression will increase your chances of recovery, but these medications do not make you sober. You still have to do the hard work of conquering your inner demons and working through rehab and a 12-step program.

We often see patients who have a physiological dependency on alcohol or narcotics. The withdrawal from these substances can be acutely painful, which makes the cravings worse and distracts from psychotherapy. With hard-core addicts, our staff of medical doctors may use specific medications to wean the body off drugs and alcohol.

Medications for Addiction Withdrawal

In addition to antidepressants, other medications can assist with the physical withdrawal symptoms of drug addiction; all of these medications are used in conjunction with talk therapy. Unlike antidepressants, these prescriptions are used primarily for a short term, until the body is able to function somewhat normally without the use of narcotics. Some of these can become addictive in themselves, so their use is closely monitored by medical doctors.

- Methadone (Dolophione) and LAAM (ORLAAM) are "replacement" drugs for those coming off opiate or heroin addictions. I find them dangerous and addictive, and I never recommend them.
- Naltrexone (Trexan) or naloxone is an "antagonist" that blocks the euphoria that results from using narcotics and reduces cravings for both drugs and alcohol.
- Buprenorphone—marketed in the United States as Suboxone and Subutex—both replaces and blocks the effects of opiates. I don't recommend using either of these, because they more or less allow the patient to remain addicted to drugs. If you are dealing with a pain-management issue, I recommend only Suboxone, because this also contains naloxone, which blocks the effects of opiates. Then we will wean the patient off Suboxone, which usually takes at least sixty days. I think these medications are too often prescribed by medical doctors who are not aware of how addicting they are. I cannot tell you how many clients I have seen totally strung out on Subutex and Suboxone, and they have to go through detox to get off them.
- Disulfiram (Antabuse) is an "aversive" drug, which makes the patient very sick if he or she drinks any alcohol.
- Bupropion (Zyban) reduces cravings for nicotine, as do Nicorette, Nicotrol, and NicoDerm.

Counselors Will Help You Determine Whether You Need Detox before Rehabilitation

The goal of a drug detox is to rid the body of toxins produced by illicit drugs and to monitor dangerous withdrawal symptoms that occur when addicts abruptly stop taking drugs. It is important for detox to be administered by medical professionals to ensure the safety of the individual and the complete elimination of the drug(s) from the body.

Addicts have numerous options in seeking a medically supervised detox. Rehab centers provide patients with medication to minimize the effects of withdrawal symptoms and maintain their physical and emotional safety. Inpatient and outpatient detox centers are available. Detox usually lasts between three and ninety days, depending on the individual's drug of choice.

Outpatient detox facilities are not effective, because the patient has easy access to scoring more drugs. Rapid detox is sometimes used with antagonist drugs to neutralize withdrawal effects, in a clinical setting with the support of medical professionals. I believe rapid detox is not effective, because some patients go back to using drugs within a week or two. This is not the time for a "quick" remedy—I have seen people die after going through a rapid detox.

Patients who have both depression and addiction should enter intense therapy, and it is also important to get plenty of exercise, eat healthy foods, change unhealthy patterns of behavior, think positively, go to a 12-step group, and take one huge dose of what I consider very important medicine for your brain: sleep. None of us ever seems to get enough. Chapter 11 contains helpful tips on improving the quality and quantity of your rest.

We don't yet have all of the exact answers to what causes addiction and alcoholism. No two patients are alike. Yet we have made great strides in the thirty years I have been in this profession, and we learn new things every day. The biggest step you can take is identifying that you have a problem. The second biggest step is taking action to address it. The things you choose to do are personal, but I have observed that many families are at a loss about where to begin I have used my experiences to shape guidelines to help you and your loved ones confront alcohol and drug addiction.

PART TWO

Recovery Solutions

5

The Hills Recovery Program

I saw some great shrinks on the long and winding road to sobriety. The options were different in the 1980s and 1990s: not a lot of professional psychiatrists were recovered addicts themselves. Or at least, they wouldn't admit it. I have been going to psychiatrists and psychologists since I was sixteen years old. When I was young, I usually felt nothing after my appointments. Sometimes I felt even worse than I did before. People tried to connect with me, but almost every time it didn't work. That's because many of them just didn't know what to do.

My colleague Jorja Davis, a therapist at the Hills, remembered the family doctor's advice she received when she went to seek help for her alcoholism, nearly thirty years ago.

"My doctor told me, 'Just stop,'" Jorja recalled. "'That's what other people do.' As if it was as easy as that!"

Historically, medical doctors have not been well equipped to provide effective treatments for addicts. I hope that your own family doctor can refer you to someone who is an expert. If not, please consult the Resources at the back of this book. This will guide you to a list of appropriate therapists near where you live.

I endured the "boot camp" of intense behavioral modification at Phoenix House because, well, that was the only type of inpatient rehab available back then. Times have changed. These days, you can rely on a powerful combination of outpatient psychotherapy, group counseling, school programs, and community support. There are now thousands of well-trained therapists who can help your loved ones.

The lessons I learned in my own treatment—and the gaps I identified—helped me become a better therapist for recovering addicts. Through years of clinical observations, I learned what works and what doesn't, when specifically treating clients with addiction or alcoholism.

As I mentioned, the best professionals are those who are recovered addicts. They will readily reveal this fact to a prospective client. If a therapist doesn't, well, then, he or she may not be the best therapist for you.

The next characteristic I identify in a good therapist is the desire and ability to form an alliance with the patient. My goal is always to create an alliance that will fight alongside you against your disease. The team will be you and me, against your beast. You and your therapist, against your beast. Two against one. You are not alone. Your therapist is on your side and will help you conquer the most shameful, damaging, humiliating problems you have.

The problem is, many addicts don't want to be part of their own team. The therapist can't form an alliance with you if you refuse to join in the fight. In my practice, I wait for my patient to join. It may

take a while before the patient is fully on board, but a good therapist will stick with the addict until both people form the alliance.

*　*　*

> I have a client named Mary who is not an addict; rather,
> she's stuck in a horrible marriage. Her husband is verbally
> abusive, and she knows it is a bad situation. But she's
> afraid of the unknown—she's never had a job, lived alone,
> or managed money. It is all I can do to encourage Mary to
> stand up and form an alliance with me, in a partnership
> that will fight for her happiness. Her demon is a fear of
> the unknown, the part of her that says, "You don't deserve
> a life of peace and happiness." I am still waiting, and I
> know Mary will join the fight eventually. She has at least
> made progress, and that's what we seek: "progress, not
> perfection." A little at a time, she is setting boundaries.

*　*　*

What also sets my program apart is that I will treat patients
even while they are still drinking or doing drugs. Many counselors and doctors refuse to see a patient until he is sober, and I find
that regretable. In almost every case, I simply "fasten my seat
belt," while the patient continues partying. I hang on for the ride.
I know it will be worth it; after all, some part of the person knows
something is wrong, because he or she has come to see me. After
a few weeks or months of therapy, we eventually reach the point
where the person is willing to change. I start to see an inkling of
self-awareness peeking through the bad craziness.

While I am on the crazy ride with the patient who is still drinking and drugging, I am still building trust with the person. I am
hanging on until he or she arrives at that psychic shift, which I
know will come. I did not have such a therapist when I was sixteen,
and if I had, it might have made a difference. My own experience
shaped me to become the therapist I am, as it has shaped Jorja

Davis and all of the other drug therapists I know. This is why it's important for addicts to find therapists who are in recovery themselves. They know the game, and they are in it for the long haul.

As a therapist, I don't actually save patients. I wait for that psychic shift, for the willingness to change. I merely provide a road map, helping them stay on course toward that moment. Sometimes, something catastrophic happens before the psychic shift—they may be hospitalized, arrested, or kicked out by their spouses. Most patients have to endure "insanity pain" before they get better. The evil demon likes to have its swan song.

•   •   •

> Mark is an eighteen-year-old alcoholic who has tried to quit drinking. He tells me he is sober, but I recognize the facade. He is acting compliant about "seeing his shrink"—as per his parents' orders—but he is still partying up a storm. I recognize the lies he is telling me (and himself). Another therapist might refuse to see such a client, but I have been through this wild ride before. After a few months, Mark will see that I am not wrong in my assessment of his behavior. He will start to believe that he and I might join forces to help bring change and meaning to his life.

•   •   •

With young patients, part of the challenge is dealing with what they think when they are *not* in the room with me. One hour per day of therapy, even every day, is not enough, because during the other twenty-three hours, their brains are working against them. In the best of all worlds, the addict or the alcoholic will receive psychotherapy five or six days a week. This is what rehab provides, whether it is an inpatient or an outpatient program.

Psychotherapy—what some people call "counseling," "talk therapy," or "behavioral therapy"—is one of the most important components in recovering from addiction (the other of which is participating in a 12-step program). I would like to emphasize that successful therapy often takes many months, sometimes even two or three years. It is a process that requires commitment and patience. The sooner you begin therapy, the sooner you will begin to heal. However, recovery begins the moment you seek treatment or attend a group meeting such as Alcoholics Anonymous. My client list is filled with people in denial. Yet still, their recovery has started, because a part of them knows there is a problem. They have sought out treatment, or they recognize that they need to be sober. Then, after they become sober, the real work begins on their deep-seated emotional issues and psychological barriers to happiness.

The first goal of my therapy program is teaching the patient the necessary skills to stop using and to avoid relapse. Addicts have, by and large, lost control over their own behavior, and most are unable to regain control without the help of someone like me. Therapists use cognitive behavioral steps to teach addicts how to cope with cravings and to prevent negative feelings that prompt the desire to get high.

My goal is to bring reality to the patient. Most of my clients in denial spend a period of time operating under the fallacy that $1 + 1 = 3$. These people are still trying to rationalize putting needles in their arms. Another one tries to rationalize taking forty Vicodin a day. That's crazy—bad crazy. I have to try to drive the point home that this person has crossed a line. Crazy is fine, but it should be good crazy. Addiction, alcoholism, lies, and rationalization are manifestations of bad crazy.

The other benefit from good therapy is that therapists are terrific at motivation. We show patients what the positive steps are and remind them of the damage that occurs when they relapse. Positive incentives and praise are helpful in changing addictive behaviors. Because recovery is a long process, the patient responds well to achieving certain milestones.

"Therapy is not what I do," says my colleague Jorja Davis. "It's who I am." Davis, like many others in recovery, refers to nonaddicted people as "normies."

"'Normie' therapists and doctors have only a few hours of training in the area of addiction," she points out. "Unlike them, we are therapists who have lived our lives steeped in the programs."

Involving family members also helps with motivation. Families who learn about the process and remain supportive throughout play an immeasurable role in successful recovery. Involvement also helps individual family members who are not the "identified patient," because addiction is a family disease. Their lives have been wrecked by the presence of an addict in the house, but they may also have contributed to the problem in the first place. Our goal is to break damaging family patterns and bring everyone back to a place of security and sanity.

Once the recovering addict is stabilized, we help him or her learn other ways to cope with stress and anxiety, find new ways to feel contentment and self-confidence, and appreciate the sensation of being happy while sober. We do this in private sessions and group therapy, and I even attend Alcoholics Anonymous meetings with my patients. AA is not therapy in itself, but a sort of community support that most counselors encourage to enhance treatment.

I am in favor of both group therapy and private counseling. Although the techniques may vary, the goal is to help addicts change their behavior, stop drinking and drugging, and start leading happy, fulfilling, productive lives. Support therapy groups are immensely helpful, because they show a patient that he or she is not alone. Addicts and alcoholics feel isolated, as if no one knows what they are going through, and group therapy shows them otherwise. This realization helps tremendously, specifically for addiction issues.

I love group therapy and see enormous gains for the patients. Groups of between six and ten people chat with one another, bringing their own experiences to help someone who is having a problem in a relationship, at school, or at work. The members of the group often provide insights that a counselor doesn't, and

I have personally gained awareness from patients for my own benefit, in these settings. Addicts and alcoholics have an innate respect for their fellow patients because they, like a therapist who is in recovery, know what it's like to struggle with the challenges of the disease. These are different from AA meetings. Although AA is a vital component in recovery, private group sessions are an additional resource for support.

* * *

In one of my groups, eighteen-year-old Gary shared that it was hard for him to spend time with his dad. His father was a successful businessman but seemed unhappy with his life and drank heavily. Gary felt obligated to cheer up his dad and tried to share helpful things with his dad that he had learned in his own therapy. He wished his father was in recovery, too. Gary's fellow group members told him that he was not responsible for his father's happiness.
"You have to look out for yourself," Sally told Gary. Sally is a recovering meth addict in her late thirties, who had left her drug-addicted husband two years earlier. "It's enough for you to keep yourself sober," she told him. "You don't have to take on his problems. He has to help himself." Gary felt relieved and a little surprised that someone in the group understood his guilt at becoming sober, while one of his family members was still using. Gary had made great strides in recovery, despite the extra challenge of problems that remained in his home. He and Sally have almost nothing in common, but their parallel paths in recovery allowed them to share tactics and sympathy in their early sobriety.

* * *

Many areas of the country have recovery therapy groups that are specifically for women or lesbians and gays, for teens, teachers, lawyers, and even doctors in recovery. Those are good, but I personally prefer the diversity of groups with a wide variety of members. Members are delighted to learn something from an unexpected source in group therapy: insight from a sober teenager may help a recovering middle-aged medical doctor, and a depressed housewife may learn coping tips from a homeless alcoholic. They have each been to hell and crawled back and have a more powerful ability to reach the soul of another addict or alcoholic.

A therapist understands that the addict's brain chemistry is going through changes. He or she also helps root out the underlying cause of insecurity or unhappiness or trauma. Many people— and not only alcoholics and addicts—are accustomed to "self-medicating" to avoid stress or uncomfortable relationships. A therapist will help reeducate the patient on how to confront problems in a sober, rational, and successful manner. The addict needs to relearn some interpersonal skills, take care of himself, and make his way in a society that still doesn't understand the disease, for the most part. In therapy, it may come to light that the patient is also suffering from a psychological ailment, such as manic depression or bipolar disorder, which can be better managed alongside his or her sobriety.

After several months or years, this patient will gain in confidence. Many patients thrive and move on from counseling, while maintaining sobriety in communities such as Alcoholics Anonymous or Narcotics Anonymous. These community meetings are an important support system for the recovering addict, but they are not the same as psychotherapy. Your loved one's specific issues need professional treatment by a therapist or a counselor, as frequently as possible, particularly at the beginning of sobriety. This is necessary not only to help the recovering addict cope with bumps in the road, relapse, and identity issues, but also to recognize the other addictions and compulsions that may rise to take the place of drugs and alcohol.

My Other Patient:
The Codependent in the Family

I mention in chapter 12 the role of codependents who are entangled in the harmful behavior when there's an addict in the house. The codependent is usually the patient's mother or father and sometimes a grandparent. The family is struggling with an addict, and often has someone who is trying to take care of the "identified patient" but is doing so in order to gratify a missing piece in him- or herself. Codependent individuals tend to ignore their own personal needs and focus on everyone else in the house. They may live vicariously through their child, basing their own emotions on how the troubled child feels that day. This becomes very unhealthy for both the codependent and the addict. Studies show that when parents are codependent like this, their children are twice as likely to become codependents themselves later in life. The child who is abusing a substance may also become codependent on the parent while actively using, thus becoming financially dependent and emotionally draining. There is some confusion about the definition or the signs of codependency. Codependency can be defined as

- Lacking a relationship with yourself; having a poor understanding of your own emotions and needs.
- Being dependent on the external. (You may try to take care of others and base your emotions on outside fixes.)
- Feeling as though you are responsible for other people's actions and emotions; being affected by other people's emotions and actions in a negative way.
- Being excessively dependent on others at the expense of yourself.
- Engaging in a continuous pattern of putting aside your needs to satisfy the needs of others.

All of these signs of codependent behavior have negative effects. Parents who are codependent are not helping their child deal with the substance abuse, and, in most situations, this further enables the child. If action is not taken, the cycle of codependency will continue. I sometimes spend as much time in therapy with family members as I do with the person who is struggling with addiction. To maximize the effects of therapy, the rest of the family must be treated for their own roles in the disease. The benefits are valuable for each of them, and the vicious cycles of anger and shame are eliminated.

The Wild Ride

I have plenty of war stories about celebrities I have treated, some of whom have stayed sober, but others still struggle with drugs and alcohol and quite publicly. I am well acquainted with the challenges of fame and wealth and the heavy party scene of admirers and groupies. The hard part of my job is that many people fail to stay in recovery. Our entire staff walks a fine line between keeping patients motivated and free of drugs and alcohol and keeping them secure, anonymous, and still engaged with outside activities. For as many success stories we have, there are some that end tragically.

I once worked with a famous television and film star who, over the years, made many trips to rehab. One of them landed him in the facility where I was working in the late 1990s. Members of his family brought him in, desperate for this young man to get help. The patient was not very cooperative, which is not unusual. His personal counselor at the facility escorted the actor to AA meetings, to the dentist and to doctor appointments for drug tests. When I learned that the counselor was driving the star to his apartment on a regular basis, "to pick up clothes," it set off an alarm for me. It turns out that celebrity patient had bribed the counselor with tens of thousands of dollars to provide drugs, prostitutes, and even to piss in a cup for him so he would pass drug tests. The counselor was still sober after twenty years but evidently was struggling with marital issues and was deeply in debt. The patient (and the counselor) had to go. Years later, this patient started personally attacking me and sent me an email in which he boasted about being off of crack for two whole weeks and declared that, next to me, "his coke dealer had more integrity." I found the situation very sad, mostly for him, of course. We hang on for the ride as long as we can, but sometimes it ends before sobriety arrives. Money and fame can be a curse, one that can prevent you from hitting bottom and changing your life.

. . .

One famous client was a wealthy retired athlete. He had millions of fans who cheered him on to championships. He'd overindulged in alcohol, cocaine, Ecstasy, marijuana, and Vicodin for twenty years. He had earned tens of millions of dollars, drove around in a Bentley, and had a private jet. Then he lost every dime he had, and suddenly he was millions of dollars in debt. By the time he landed in our rehab center, this sports star had been charged with several crimes and was awaiting sentencing. Although he remained sober, he was in denial about many issues during the ninety days I spent working with him. He understood that he was an addict but still blamed his problems on other people. I knew it would take several months to penetrate the arrogance and denial, but I never got the chance, because he was sentenced to prison for several years. Ninety days was not enough. This was a guy who had come from nothing to achieve the American dream. Yet he had based his life on money, fame, and power and, thanks to his addictions, never established a basic foundation of integrity, family responsibility, and self-esteem. I lived in that world once. I, too, had everything and was putting a needle in my arm at age sixteen. I am so lucky.

You know what? That failed example is a lucky one.
He is still alive. It still breaks my heart to remember
Chris Farley, the comedian from *Saturday Night Live*. He
was an outrageous personality—I admired him as Matt
Foley from *SNL*, the guy "who lived in a van, down by
the river." Farley had recently hit it big in several successful movies such as *Black Sheep* and *Tommy Boy*. In fact,
he had just been hired to voice the main character in a
new animated movie called *Shrek*. I was the program
director at another facility when Farley checked in during
the late 1990s. He was, at age thirty-two, addicted to
food, alcohol, cocaine, opiates—well, you name it. He
checked in for our recovery program because his family
and friends had urged him to do so, which is a common
scenario.

Farley was a fun-loving patient who loved to act out.
One time he located the main power box for the whole
rehab center and shut it down, sending staff members in
a frenzy to locate patients and find the problem with the
power source. He hid in a closet and could not be found,
then pounced out onto a staff member in the dark and ran
away, completely naked, screaming hysterically. Another
time we took a group of patients to the beach. Farley
stripped off all of his clothes and ran around naked,
prancing in the water, while staff members tried to contain his antics in front of a hundred onlookers. Farley had
frequent meltdowns and started to physically threaten
staff members. This was all while he was sober, mind you,
and off drugs for a couple of months. His demons were
severe. He was accustomed to acting out and being the
center of attention and would not even begin to talk about
his many issues. Farley couldn't even sit still; he was
uncomfortable in his own skin. He created drama and
spectacles because of his deep anger and sadness. It

seemed to me that he had a big hole inside, which caused him enormous pain. It was extremely frustrating for all of us at the center who spent many weeks trying to reach him. But Farley simply wasn't finished with his wild ride; amazingly, he had not yet hit "bottom."

Ultimately, Chris was so disruptive that he was taking attention away from other patients and interfering with their treatment. I finally had to tell him that other patients felt unsafe around him, and I asked him to leave. It is common to ask patients to leave if they are found using drugs or alcohol repeatedly, but that's not what happened with Chris. He wasn't using; he was simply uncontainable and had come no closer to dealing with his issues, after many weeks of therapy. He had been sober many weeks when he left rehab but was no closer to recovery than he had been before he got there. He clearly had a big hole inside. I never saw him again. Within a couple months, he was dead from a drug overdose.

· · ·

It never gets easier to see patients who have the best of intentions slip away. It is the hardest part of our job, but such is the nature of this disease. Relapse is common, and failure is high. Those who work in this field acknowledge that there are long odds and countless obstacles to success. When you are a therapist who is in recovery himself, however, you know more than the average doctor about this beast. Therapists who are in recovery don't give up on a patient. If the patient disappears on a bender, we welcome his or her eventual return, with no judgments. I am thrilled when patients who have relapsed come back to my office, weeks or months later, even if they are still using. Their very presence shows me that they have acknowledged a problem.

Find yourself a therapist who will put on a seat belt, if necessary, and hang on for the ride.

6

Fallback Addictions

After the amazing feat of conquering substance or alcohol addiction, you may find that a new compulsive behavior is waiting to take its place. It may be less dangerous, even legal or socially acceptable, but it is equally threatening when it comes to the quality of your life. I sometimes call it "Beast 2.0."

I was living sober in Los Angeles at age thirty-eight, and I decided, with my experience at NYU Film School, to go into the movie business. How I managed to hang on to sobriety in the industry most known for drinking and drugging is beyond me. Yet even though I managed to stay off drugs and booze, I found myself acting compulsively in another way: with a "love addiction."

Whenever I felt insecure or uncomfortable, I got "fixed" by women. It was my drug of choice, and I used it as a sort of validation. I would fall madly in love, feeling euphoric and invincible. In reality, unbeknownst to me, this was caused by past traumas and residual pain from childhood. I think my mother had a similar addiction—the fallacy of a knight in shining armor, that love would rescue her from all of the bad things in life. Long after my dad left my mother, she waited for him to return, and it essentially destroyed her life. So I would fall in love with one fascinating woman after another, all of whom were carrying around mountains of baggage and issues of their own. Yet it always ended in devastation. Not only was I picking the wrong women, but, because I was merely replacing one addiction with another, I was picking them for all of the wrong reasons. Pia Mellody wrote a terrific book that helped me, called *Facing Love Addiction*, which I highly recommend.

Often we attach ourselves to some other compulsion to replace the primary addiction. Some of us need to obsess about seemingly anything, as if our lives depended on it. Smoking cigarettes, having a lot of sex, gambling, overeating, Internet pornography, and even excessive exercise can cover up residual sadness or issues that once drove us to drink or use drugs. This is because, even now that you're sober, you may still not be cleared of the emotional issues that started you down that road in the first place. After physiological recovery, you need to begin the psychological healing. Psychotherapy is typically not effective until you reach sobriety. The reason you used alcohol or cocaine or heroin in the first place is that anything is better than confronting that inner evil.

Make no mistake: compulsive behaviors such as gambling and eating disorders are addictions, in and of themselves. Although you may believe the second addiction is not as bad as the first one, it clearly indicates that you are not yet healed from the psychological issues that started you off on the first addiction. Someone who recovers from one of these as his primary addiction may turn to alcohol or drugs as his fallback, instead of the other way around.

• • •

My patient Josie displays another example of Addiction
2.0. She is twenty-seven and recovering from heroin
and alcohol addiction. She has made great progress,
attends AA meetings, and is coming into a new sense of
self-awareness, learning about her authentic self in
sobriety. Yet whenever she fails to find a way to express
her feelings these days, she gets a razor and cuts her
forearm. This cutting brings her a sense of relief, a
twisted outlet that expresses her frustration and confusion. That's another form of addiction. Josie's overwhelming sadness and anger are still self-destructive,
quite literally in her case. One day she came to her regular appointment, and I learned that she had put staples
in her leg. This was basically behavior on the edge of
relapse.

"No," I said. "That's self-destructive, and it has to
stop." She got angry, stood up, and left my office. Josie's
demons kept on going. When Josie's roommate arrived
home to find a suicide note, she called the police. Josie
was found at a bar, drunk, and one of her sober companions went to pick her up. Josie was angry, out of control,
and jumped through the window when the car was going
thirty-five miles an hour. She was taken to the hospital
and, fortunately, was only a little banged up. Josie has no
recollection of any of these events, and she subsequently
entered the inpatient rehab center.

• • •

Josie's cutting is a compulsive behavior pattern that rein-
forces the disease, which then easily leads to relapse with drugs
and alcohol. This is the sort of residual shock wave in sobriety
that a good therapist will ride through, again "wearing a seat

belt." Josie is still in therapy, and we continue to work on the issues that she had transferred into cutting. She feels that people still don't understand her, and she is proud of her offbeat characteristics that set her apart. I am working with her to use less crazy ways to express this "wild" part of her nature, to put it to positive use in her life, instead of expressing it in destructive ways. I'm all in favor of good crazy.

•   •   •

Another example of a fallback addiction is the case of Betty Jo, who is recovering from a serious crystal meth habit. She is a stunning fashion model, who used her substance abuse to maintain the excruciatingly thin physique that her profession required. Betty Jo spent ninety days in rehab at the Hills and then started to see me for therapy twice a week. During the course of a year, she emerged free of meth addiction, as well as alcohol and all drugs. Yet she had become particularly sensitive about her diet, to the point where she now had a full-blown eating disorder. Betty Jo was meticulously tracking microcalories and working out at the gym five hours a day, seven days a week. Once she recognized that she had a new addiction, Betty Jo and I worked on how she could express her feelings in other ways. She learned to play tennis, which she now loves. This is an activity where she can apply her obsessive mind to game strategies and perfecting her backhand. It's an activity that involves interaction with other people, and she loves the challenge of a Round Robin now, instead of creating her own impossible goals on the weight machines. She also consulted a nutritionist to relieve herself from compulsively micromanaging everything she ate.

•   •   •

This early stage in sobriety and the arrival of a fallback addiction are times when therapists may discover that the patient has underlying manic depression or bipolar disorder. This is commonly unrecognized until after the addict is sober. It's hard to diagnose someone who is as high as a kite. Even if these psychological conditions are being treated, however, this does not mean that people are not still addicts. They are. Taking a Zoloft does not mean they can go back to drinking "socially." They are still addicts with a dual diagnosis, but both can be managed, and they can find enormous happiness and self-fulfillment.

The Dry Drunk

In some cases, the recovered addict will be doing well in sobriety, yet will still act out in negative ways, even though the person is not drinking or using drugs. "Dry drunk" is really a misnomer, because the person is not a drunk, but it's what we sometimes call the patient who hasn't yet addressed his or her underlying psychological issues. Similar to people who become addicted to a replacement compulsion, this recovering addict still remains in isolation and denial and is incapable of becoming truly fulfilled.

•   •   •

A patient named Martha came to me because of issues with her husband, J.R. He had quit drinking three years earlier and was doing well, attending AA meetings, and staying with the program. But J.R. had stopped going to therapy immediately upon getting sober. He disappeared for hours at a time, remaining separate from family activities with their children. Martha couldn't help being fearful, and their children could sense it, which threw off the household dynamic as if J.R. were still drinking. Sure, J.R. was clean and sober, but he was a mess inside.

He was acting resentful toward Martha, for one, and was impatient with the children, acting as if they were a great burden to him. I advised her that J.R. was probably regretful that he had failed the family and himself, perhaps also falling short of his life dreams. He had wasted twenty years of his life, lost in the fog of alcoholism, and was probably still afraid of confronting real life. He was also feeling sorry for himself, evidently. He refused to come in for therapy, and Martha was walking on eggshells.

"I don't want him to squash the joy of life for our kids," she told me. "I want them to know that they can be successful, in spite of J.R. acting like everything's a drag." We discussed ways she could remain aware and vigilant of her own emotions and those of her children, knowing that J.R. may never change his negative attitude or chart his own path to happiness. She also weighed the options of ending her marriage, which she has not yet pursued. Martha goes to Al-Anon meetings and has brought her children in to me for counseling as well.

J.R.'s "fallback addiction" was in not completing the important step of therapy. He thought he could become sober all on his own. His addiction is remaining angry and resentful at the world, which "took away" his ability to drink, while he avoids addressing the underlying causes of his initial problem with drinking. If he refuses to seek professional help or to attend support meetings, he will remain in that fallback addiction, "white-knuckling" it as a dry drunk. If he remains sober, then at least he can provide for his family and bring them less harm. However, if he does not do the painful work of identifying and addressing his emotional challenges, then he will not reach his authentic self.

The only person he harms is himself. Well, actually, the dry drunk ultimately harms his friends and family, too. The relapse rate for a dry drunk is extremely high, as you might expect. Whether the problem was with alcohol or opiates or marijuana, these patients have a false sense of control, the hallmark denial that signals they are still "addicted."

How to Beat Your TV or Internet Addiction

- Give your extra TVs to charity. Keep only one.
- Turn on the TV only to watch a particular show. In other words, don't just turn it on and go surfing for something worthwhile.
- Throw out the TV remote control. Yes, it can be done.
- Put your TV and computer monitor at inconvenient angles in the room, or hide them completely in cabinets.
- Do not eat food while on the computer or while watching TV.
- If the sun is shining, go outdoors. Go for a walk or a bike ride. Get a dog!
- Read ten pages of a newspaper, a magazine, or a book before you turn on the power.
- Do not allow yourself to watch endlessly repeating series or marathons.

7

Shedding the Shame and Guilt

For the first thirty-two years of my life, I did not deal with my underlying insecurities. I used drugs and a sense of entitlement and arrogance to cover up my insecure feelings. I have six sisters and one brother, and I was never as smart or self-confident as they were. I had wonderful parents and magnificent opportunities that very few people are lucky enough to have, but it was never enough to compensate for my feelings of failure. Now, we can't pin blame on any one thing or another, in any event. Many people can rise above far worse conditions to reach success and happiness. Yet I know now that I was suffering from a chemical imbalance and dyslexia, during the heady 1960s when young people were introduced to recreational drug experimentation. Back then, my parents were preoccupied with many things and were often not at home.

The root causes of addiction are so many things: dysfunctional families, physical abuse, sexual abuse, violence or trauma,
learning disabilities, chemical imbalance, emotional problems.
For many, it is simply a genetic code that was handed to you.
There should be no shame or guilt associated with these things,
and I am here to say that you can change how you feel. These are
all issues that can't be fixed by other parts of our society. The
government's not going to fix your family crisis. Congress is not
going to pass a law that remedies the emotional abuse you suffered at the hands of a terrible spouse or parent. The interesting
thing about residual shame and guilt over addiction is that they
occur not only in the identified patient—the addict or the
alcoholic—but they also occur in the rest of the family members.
A therapist who is treating a family in recovery will focus on
eradicating the guilt and the shame that have been embedded in
the dynamic for everyone.

Guilt is when we tell ourselves, "I did a bad thing." Any of us
who have cheated on our spouses feel guilt over our behavior.
Any of us who have stolen a towel from a hotel might feel a pang
of guilt. Guilt is a very common emotion for someone who goes
out all night snorting coke on a bar crawl. Yet guilt sometimes
causes us to do positive things. Guilt might even be the thing
that gets us to enter treatment. Yet it is not as dangerous as feeling shame.

Shame goes deeper; shame is when we tell ourselves, "I am a
bad person." Long-term repeated feelings of guilt create shame—
listening to years of our parents bickering and blaming ourselves
or hurting someone else's feelings by getting drunk every night.
It is our sense of shame that turns us into addicts, and then we
maintain the shame with our addictions.

Shame, like alcoholism and addiction, makes us feel powerless, isolated, unworthy, and secretive. We feel weak and out of
control, and we are ashamed of this weakness, which intensifies

our neediness and sometimes drives us into relapse. Some of us may have parents who belittled us and raised us to have a poor self-image, an internal sense that we are unworthy of love or respect. Perhaps you have a spouse who belittles you and constantly puts you down. We start to repeat these thoughts to ourselves, cementing the idea that we are bad people. Our sense of shame grows and becomes organic to our systems, and then we shut down emotionally or start to act out inappropriately. As we become sober, we need to dislodge that embedded sense of shame, that underlying bullshit that creates a vicious cycle.

Here's the good news: shame can be conquered. In fact, it must be conquered before you reach your sense of fulfillment and your authentic good crazy self. Shame is a learned behavior, and it can be unlearned. A therapist will guide you toward the positive aspects of your life and will remind you how to feel gratitude for everything in your life that is not shameful. We learn how to cope with our fears so that they don't "morph" into shame and how to overcome fear so that we connect with other people. While we were in the throes of alcohol and drugs, we didn't give much thought to other people. We hid our problem and stayed isolated, fearing that our shame would be exposed. Forming bonds with others can eliminate shame, which is why I'm such a proponent of community groups like AA, which I'll discuss in the next chapter. When we feel connected to other people, we start to feel compassion, not only for others but for ourselves. The greatest cure for shame is caring for others and allowing them to care for us, warts and all. No one is perfect, but you can love who you are, just as you love others who are less than perfect. Loving and being loved bring a high that is far more exhilarating than doing drugs.

Don't be ashamed of who you are. Stop fearing what other people think about you. Stand up and say, "I am an addict," or "I am a manic depressive." Come out of the closet. It is not your fault. No one should blame you for your disease. Stand tall and take responsibility for your life. I cannot stand to see clients shamed about their drug use or alcoholism—not by family members, coworkers, teachers, or doctors. Addiction and alcoholism carry a huge stigma in our society. Shame can destroy someone who is doing well in recovery—she sometimes feels as if she cannot unload that burden, that horrible "secret." If someone in your life is reinforcing the negative mantra and making you feel ashamed, then please stay away from him or her. Move out, and move on. Enablers may not even know they are adding to your sense of shame, but if you recognize it, then sever the ties. When you become like an open book, as I have, then there is no more underlying bullshit to keep the cycle of shame going. I am what I am. You are what you are. I am proud of you for getting this far.

Writing

Not everyone is a writer, but keeping a journal is a huge help in learning how to express your feelings, sharing them with others (or not), and learning how to read between the lines. Going to group therapy meetings often includes reading from your journal. It acts as a "cheat sheet" when you share stories from your daily life. As you get accustomed to jotting down a few notes at the end of a day or the beginning of your day, you will be amazed at how the passing comments start to shape into patterns and insights that you would otherwise overlook or forget.

It doesn't have to be a special notebook or diary. Use your laptop or tablet; use your cell phone to send yourself text messages. Draw pictures, bookmark Web clips, make lists with bullets. "Writing" is more like "recording your thoughts," for our purposes, and can take whatever form is easiest for you. You don't even have to share these thoughts with others, if you choose not to. It is still a helpful daily exercise, even for simply sorting out thoughts in your own head.

I have included lengthy exercises for writing in chapter 9 of this book, and they are also available for printing out at www.thehillscenter.com.

The Disease of More

In my practice, I see many people who are very success-ful. Mark is a Wall Street trader who has more money than God. He started out with nothing, and, after a few years of working hard in finance, he attained huge wealth. He also developed an appetite to become more and more successful, even though he had reached the pinnacle of the industry. His business coups and the respect from his industry peers were never enough. So "more and more" for Mark turned into more women, more alcohol, and more cocaine. He tried heroin and didn't like it, so he merely continued doing an eight-ball of coke a day. If he could have done "more," he would have. The next day, of course, he always felt totally alone, empty, sick, and depressed. He wanted more, of some-thing, of anything.

· · ·

I often see patients who have absolutely everything: fame, money, family, career. Yet it's almost as if they become spiritually polluted. The parties are everywhere, the money is flowing, they even have movie star fame and a loving family, but nothing is enough. These people are still looking for more, even when they have so much. I call it the "Disease of More," and I hope that one day it is given more awareness and somehow eradicated or at least beaten down to controllable levels. This means that we would all know that it is our actions and our connections with others that bring our lives value.

. . .

Another patient, Candy, is addicted to Adderall and meth. Her parents give her a credit card for anything she wants: a Range Rover, Prada accessories, Tiffany jewelry. This evidently serves to appease her parents' own sense of shame, but what her parents are providing Candy with is the express-lane route to the Disease of More. She was taught that she can have anything she wants, which makes it all the harder for both of us to cope with her wanting more and more drugs. Specifically, coke, Ecstasy, and marijuana, mixed with vodka and Red Bull. She has all the money in the world, and she is a miserable mess. Her parents showered her with things in a misguided attempt to help her, to give Candy what they didn't have when they were young. Instead, they have provided her with an endless stream of mindless consumption in her search for identity and fulfillment, leaving Candy with a distorted definition of happiness that has utterly failed her. The parents will not join us at Candy's counseling sessions, but I am still hopeful they will one day join in their daughter's struggle toward sobriety.

. . .

In our society, in all Western cultures, everything is about bigger, better, faster. We rely on external things to define us. We all want more. Yet all we really need are shelter, food, air, and water. Maybe you need a nice dog or a garden to work in. I don't say that to be funny. Therapist Jorja Davis reminds our patients that monks who chop wood and carry water do so for a reason: repetitive action, even petting a dog or a cat, releases endorphins and serotonin in our brains. It feels good. We don't need the newest Audi. We don't need a bottle of tequila that costs two hundred dollars. We don't need an amethyst credit card that buys us more crap. We need a sense of self-worth, one that comes without price tags, and is not based on the value of our possessions.

If there was one thing I would change in our society—other than outlawing recreational drugs, of course, which is and will continue to be a nightmare for many years—it would be how we teach our children. We need to end this epidemic of the Disease of More. Even if you don't have children, pay attention to what is going on around you. Ask yourself how you can make a difference to someone whose values are screwed up. Make a list of what you truly cherish in your life. If any of these can be replaced by spending money, then you are living with confused priorities. See if you can change the way you think. Spend a week or two in retreat, chopping wood, carrying water. Volunteer at a homeless shelter; mentor a school kid from the other side of town.

Less is more. Less stuff is more. Less shame is more, too. You can be free of these attachments and feel lighter, freer, and ready to step forward into self-fulfillment.

Be Grateful

Here's what we need more of: gratitude. No one actively practices it anymore, it seems. We make long lists of our grievances (including our addictions) but too few lists of all of the things for which we should give thanks. We should be grateful for our families, even dysfunctional ones, because they at least put up with all of our bullshit. We should feel glad to see the beauty of a sunrise, when we're not too loaded to feel the warmth as it hits our skin. We should be grateful for the fact that we are still alive, since some of us have lost a few friends along the way. We should be happy that we can start anew, beginning today, to change our attitude and make the world a better place. We have so many choices in our lives. That, in itself, is something to be thankful for.

I mention Viktor Frankl in chapter 3. He was a psychiatrist who survived a Nazi concentration camp. When he was liberated, he could have spent a lifetime feeling victimized and isolated. He chose another way: gratitude.

Frankl wrote, "Everything can be taken from a man or a woman but one thing: the last of human freedoms to choose one's attitude in any given set of circumstances, to choose one's own way." If it worked for him, it can work for you. I know that it works for me.

I think feeling grateful makes you empowered over your own life. Being thankful naturally leads to thoughts of how to best use such blessings in your life; it leads to goal setting and a desire to share the feeling with someone else. If you don't feel grateful, you wallow in a sense of feeling victimized—and you aren't a victim anymore. Be thankful, at least, for that.

8

The Value of Support Groups

Imagine a network of people whose primary goal is to welcome you, accept you as you are, listen to your problems, offer help with voices that echo your own experience, refer you to job interviews, and perhaps help you find a place to live, who support you against common daily obstacles and praise you for all of the positive things you bring to the world. Imagine that this network spans the globe and meets in every community, in every country, on a daily basis, several times a day, so that you can always find a group, and it never costs money. This group of people understands where you've been and where you're going, even if you've never met them before, even if you don't speak the same language. It is still astonishing to me that every community in the world has a group that will help support your recovery.

The benefits of such groups are immeasurable and quite important to your success. I don't care if it's a 12-step philosophy such as Alcoholics Anonymous, a recovery community based on *A Course in Miracles*, a local church group, meetings of people who study the writings of Eckhart Tolle or a group that follows the Koran, Buddhism, or the Bible: they serve the same purpose, providing community support with members who have the same problems that you do. You cannot recover by yourself, in isolation. You simply can't do it alone. It takes a village, someone who is there for you, 24/7.

The only way you can stay sober is through a "connection." When you don't have a connection, you are alone, just you and your mind. The disease will pick you off in no time. It is vital for us to go to recovery meetings three or four times a week, to bind with the people who are like us. We have a commonality, almost like war veterans back from Afghanistan. We're all crazy, but it's the good crazy. Many of us have a dark sense of humor, but it helps us stay sane and keeps us coming back.

To illustrate the importance of community as a component of recovery, I discuss the benefits of Alcoholics Anonymous in particular. But let me clarify: it need not be Alcoholics Anonymous (AA) for you. If you have access to another community group that provides you with support in sobriety, then I heartily approve. For most people, however, AA is the most readily available— whether you are a wealthy industrialist hooked on Vicodin or an unemployed single mom addicted to crack. In other words, Alcoholics Anonymous is everywhere and does not restrict itself only to members addicted to alcohol.

Alcoholics Anonymous

Bill Wilson was a raging alcoholic who founded Alcoholics Anonymous in 1935. Wilson and his partner, Dr. Bob Smith, developed the "Twelve Traditions" in 1946 to unify the program across the country. These traditions recommend that the group members remain anonymous, that they help other alcoholics, and that they welcome anyone who wishes to quit drinking or using drugs. AA steers clear of religious dogma and involvement in public issues and is endorsed by the American Psychiatric Association to help treat the disease of addiction. The fellowship was expanded with groups such as Narcotics Anonymous, Cocaine Anonymous, and so forth, which adhere to the same twelve traditions. As stated previously, any kind of addict is welcome at any of these meetings.

Bill W. claimed, "We must find some spiritual basis for living, else we die." Now, I am not a very religious man, so I didn't begin my sobriety by attending AA meetings. The concept of a "higher power" had turned me off. I thought AA was "God this, God that," similar to going to church. I was wrong, and it was just dumb luck that enabled me to stay sober during that period without the support of a community. It took me a while to realize that AA invokes the "higher power" of your understanding, whatever your understanding might be. You get to determine what your higher power is.

For me, the definition arrived on the Upper West Side of Manhattan, in a story I mentioned in the introduction. I was thirty-four years old and sitting on a stoop in New York City with that sixteen-year-old who really wanted to go out and get loaded. I was working for Phoenix House, talking to this kid, trying to help him connect with his authentic self. He broke down and sobbed, and I recognized myself in the young man. He worked through the pain and fear and started to express his frustration and stopped feeling the need to get high. He let go of that huge knot inside, on that day, and found peace. He did not go out and self-medicate. I experienced a spiritual moment that was visceral. I felt an enormous sense of transcendence, being part of the cathartic process that helped this young man. It was something I wanted to feel again, the way I once wanted to get high.

It dawned on me, then, that this was my higher power. It wasn't "God," as many people might think of it. For me, the higher power was the sensation of sitting on that stoop with a sixteen-year-old on the Upper West Side, who didn't get loaded that day. The feeling inside me was transformative. Helping others became my higher power. That was how I felt spiritual. Helping others is my truth, my authentic self. That is my higher power, to this day. "God" is just a catchword for those in recovery. It need not be a single entity or an omnipotent being. When I finally identified my higher power, I started going to AA meetings. I am forever grateful for the insight that brought me there, for the powerful connection of these friends and strangers who have provided unconditional support.

No one judges you in AA. If you go out and get drunk, they welcome you back the next day, to start again. If you have a problem with believing that God is your "higher power," do not use that as a reason to reject this—or any—12-step program. Many members choose to use the group itself as their "higher power." The 12 steps or Mother Earth can be considered your higher power. Sobriety can be your higher power.

Some people object to the AA credo that states members should admit that they are "powerless" over alcohol. I don't have a problem with that, because I see patients every day who show me how powerless they are against drugs and alcohol. If that word bothers you, don't let it stop you from gaining all of the benefits AA can bring to you. To me, "powerless" means I cannot be my own higher power. It took me twenty years as an addict before I figured out that I could not control my consumption of drugs and alcohol, as hard as I tried to. I am powerless over it. I have power over many other things: my free will, my conscience, my friends, my faith, my integrity, my life, and even my sobriety. But I do not have power over my addictive tendencies. In order to maintain my powers of volition and self-fulfillment, I use the

AA community to resist the one thing over which I have no power: addiction. It works.

One of the best things about AA—or any similar support group—is the wild variety of personalities who belong, such as the ones I have come to know and love. Where else would I become great friends with a street musician and a famous writer? So many former addicts have the best sense of humor—the dark, edgy humor that comes from the trenches of battle. The one who offers the most enlightened snippet of support may be a person you never would have met anywhere else. One of my favorite groups meets in downtown Los Angeles on Mondays. It's filled with hip young artists and college students. Going to a meeting is more fun than happy hour at a comedy club. Not all of the groups are like that. I still go to another group on Wednesdays where the members are a little older (and well-to-do). How would I know the power of this group if I hadn't personally witnessed the miracles that have occurred within its walls? Patients can recover in these "rooms," stay sober, and work through issues to find happiness. We are all in this together, people helping people, with no judgments.

I have a friend who is a "normie," a nonaddict, who was encountering a lot of issues in her home life and at work. She turned to me and said, "I wish I were in recovery, so I could belong to a support group like AA."

It's easy to find a meeting, no matter where you live or wherever you may be traveling. Look it up in the local phone book or on the Internet. Sometimes the meetings are advertised in the classified ads in newspapers and on Craigslist.com. If you need a ride, call the telephone contact. No matter where you attend an AA meeting, you will never reveal your last name, and you need never say a word at all, if you choose not to. Recovery begins when you attend a meeting. Even after a relapse, you can begin again the next day.

If your loved one goes to treatment but is not attending 12-step meetings on a regular basis, that person is on the path to relapse. Help yourself by finding a local Al-Anon meeting, the program specifically designed for people with a loved one who is an alcoholic or an addict.

Because I don't use God as my "higher power," the 12 steps I follow look somewhat different than the traditional steps. For me, the higher power is my truth and my authentic self, that spiritual feeling when I help another person work through the pain and fear of addiction. It will be unique to you, if you also invoke a higher power other than God. This is my version of the program that essentially is my mantra in life:

1. We admitted we were powerless over alcohol—that our lives had become unmanageable.
2. Came to believe that a Power greater than ourselves could restore us to sanity.
3. Made a decision to turn our will and our lives over to the care of *our truths and our authentic selves.*
4. Made a searching and fearless moral inventory of ourselves.
5. Admitted to *our authentic selves* and to another human being the exact nature of our wrongs.
6. Were entirely ready to have *our truths and our authentic selves* remove all of these defects of character.
7. Humbly asked *our truths and our authentic selves* to remove my shortcomings.
8. Made a list of all persons we had harmed, and became willing to make amends to them all.
9. Made direct amends to such people wherever possible, except when doing so would injure them or others.

10. Continued to take personal inventory and, when we were wrong, promptly admitted it.

11. Sought through prayer and meditation to improve our conscious contact with *our truths and our authentic selves*, praying only for knowledge of *their* will for me and the power to carry that out.

12. Having had a spiritual awakening as the result of these Steps, we tried to carry this message to *others* and to practice these principles in all our affairs.

In my mind, the most important step is the first step. It's the only way to have long-term sobriety, in which your life can really change. I remind myself on a daily basis who the enemy is: the drugs and the drink. You have to know that the drugs and the drink are the demon that has destroyed your life. The day you forget that is the day you lose your sobriety.

I have so many clients who come into my office, and they recognize they are addicts in an intellectual way but not in an emotional way. They have not yet emotionally connected to their "bottom." My bottom is seared into my memory: the visualization of the time when I knocked on my mother's apartment door, and when she opened the door, she looked at me with an expression of abject fear. Because of all of the pain I had caused her, she was afraid of her own son. When I remember the look on her face, it was as if I was a demon to her. I think of that moment, and it has kept me sober for twenty-eight years.

When you have a moment like that in your own life, then you will truly commit to the first step. Perhaps you can envision all of the people you have hurt and truly know who your enemy is. When I see a client who doesn't feel that bottom—even though intellectually she knows she has a problem—then I know she will go out and get loaded again. So, without question, we spend the most time and effort on that first step. You need to truly surrender, in an emotional way. When you realize you are power-less over your addiction, you will begin to find humility. I was finally able to surrender. I still do it: I literally get on my knees and bow my head to the floor. When I'm talking in my groups, I get down on the floor and bow. Humility can be empowering, and, because you are powerless over the addiction, it feels good to find power in something else.

Alcoholics and addicts who can't truly commit to the first step are letting arrogance and grandiosity get in the way. As a result, they are still weak, vulnerable to the beast of addiction.

· · ·

One of my clients was sober for nine months. Twenty-nine-year-old James came to see me regularly for coun-seling, but it was clear he hadn't surrendered. He hadn't committed to the first step. He knew he was addict, logi-cally and intellectually, but he was still lying and manipu-lating his family members for money and keeping secrets. I told him repeatedly that he had not yet emotionally sur-rendered and that he would get loaded again. I could see through his lies and manipulation, and he wasn't chang-ing his behavior. After nine months of being sober, he went out on a drug run and disappeared on a bender of Oxy and benzos.

James came back a few weeks later. He comes in now, and he's sober, but he's still manipulating friends and fam-ily for money and telling lies, feeling no guilt or responsi-bility for his behavior. He's still spending his parents' money without their knowledge and openly admits he can't be trusted. Obviously, he has issues about his family, and he resents how they have "taken things away" from him. Yet he hasn't recognized that he put himself in this situa-tion. No one "did" anything to him; he did it all to himself.

"I know what you're doing," I tell him. "You haven't surrendered the behavior, so you going to relapse again." Until he opens up about his inner conflicts, he will continue on this path of insanity. He has been sober for three months now and goes to AA meetings, even has a sponsor. Yet as the old ad used to say, "What's real and what's Memorex?" James is just going through the motions because he has to.

"Total surrender means you take your secrets and expose them," I tell James. "Then you will get everything in life that you want. You will no longer need to rely on manipulation as if it were a drug."

⁎　⁎　⁎

If you can truly commit to the first step, the other eleven steps will fall into place for you. You will start to work through the actual issues that led you to addiction, and you will more easily cope with any repercussions, intimacy issues, or secondary addictions that may arrive.

You might even need to move farther away from your family members. When people arrive in rehab from distant places, they often do much better, simply because their dysfunctional families are not around. I don't recommend that you totally cut yourself off from your family, unless there was serious abuse in your case. Yet sometimes it is very effective to move to a new location and re-create a new "family" who is healthier for you. I love the vibrant community of recovery in LA, and I know other patients who have found happiness in similar hip and sober communities, such as Minneapolis, south Florida, New York, and San Francisco. Of course, there are sober communities in every town. Recovery is a social movement found around the world. Everyone in this country, addicted or not, would benefit from a community life as rich as the recovery movement.

When you commit to the first step, your worst nightmare becomes the idea of going back to your addiction. When I remember my mother's face all of those years ago, I make a daily commitment to the first step.

Alateen

Many young adults are confused and angry about their family members' drinking and drugging. Teenagers have a great resource for finding support and learning how to live with and love a family member in recovery. It's a perfect group for young siblings or children of addicts.

Alateen is a fellowship of young Al-Anon members whose lives have been affected by someone else's drinking or drug use. As in AA, young people between the ages of thirteen and nineteen get together to share their experiences, strengths, and hopes with one another. They discuss the difficulties of living with a family member who is suffering from alcoholism or addiction, they learn how to effectively cope with the problems they face, and they encourage and help one another to understand the principles outlined by Al-Anon and apply the 12 steps and traditions toward improving their emotional lives.

By attending meetings once a week, Alateens learn that compulsive drinking and drug use are not vindictive actions that their loved ones take in order to hurt them but are a progressive illness. Members of Alateen also come to understand that they are not the cause of their loved ones' substance abuse and addictive behaviors; they have no control over these actions, but they do have control over how they respond to them. In doing so, young Alateens also learn that they have the option to detach emotionally from their loved ones' substance abuse, while continuing to love and support them. Alateens are afforded the spiritual and intellectual resources to maintain a relationship with someone who suffers from alcoholism and drug addiction, as well as to develop their own potential as individuals and to build satisfying and rewarding life experiences through a strong foundation of fellowship.

In finding a home in Alateen, young people, similar to the adult alcoholics and addicts they love, have the opportunity to relate to other people their age whose home lives are similar. The environment of sharing fosters a healthy learning experience from which to grow emotionally, and it provides hope. They enter adulthood with minds that have been broadened by acceptance and understanding, and they can reap the benefits of a new life in which they are accepted and understood.

Other Special Groups

Other demographic groups prefer communities of people who have the exact same addiction or situation, but it is not necessary in order to benefit from the support of a community of addicts, period. Many times, it is easier to locate an AA meeting, and you are welcome in any meeting, no matter what your substance of choice. Other times, the atmosphere or the attendees of one group are different from what you may prefer—so choose another group to attend. You will gain more benefits from the one in which you feel most comfortable.

Here are some of the groups that follow a variation of the 12 steps. Most of these can be found in every community in the nation and around the globe.

- AA: Alcoholics Anonymous
- ACA or ACOA: Adult Children of Alcoholics
- Al-Anon/Alateen: for friends and family members of alcoholics
- CA: Cocaine Anonymous

- CLA: Clutterers Anonymous
- CMA: Crystal Meth Anonymous
- Co-Anon: for friends and family of addicts
- CoDA: Co-Dependents Anonymous, for people working to end patterns of dysfunctional relationships and develop functional and healthy relationships
- COSA: formerly Codependents of Sex Addicts
- COSLAA: CoSex and Love Addicts Anonymous
- DA: Debtors Anonymous
- EA: Emotions Anonymous, for recovery from mental and emotional illness
- EHA: Emotional Health Anonymous, for recovery from mental and emotional illness
- FA: Families Anonymous, for relatives and friends of addicts
- FA: Food Addicts in Recovery Anonymous
- FAA: Food Addicts Anonymous
- GA: Gamblers Anonymous
- Gam-Anon/Gam-A-Teen: for friends and family members of problem gamblers
- HA: Heroin Anonymous
- MA: Marijuana Anonymous
- NA: Narcotics Anonymous
- NAIL: Neurotics Anonymous, for recovery from mental and emotional illness
- Nar-Anon: for friends and family members of addicts
- NicA: Nicotine Anonymous
- OA: Overeaters Anonymous
- OLGA: Online Gamers Anonymous
- PA: Pills Anonymous, for recovery from prescription pill addiction

- SA: Sexaholics Anonymous
- SA: Smokers Anonymous
- SAA: Sex Addicts Anonymous
- SCA: Sexual Compulsives Anonymous
- SIA: Survivors of Incest Anonymous
- SLAA: Sex and Love Addicts Anonymous
- WA: Workaholics Anonymous

Sponsors

The other valuable resource in groups such as Alcoholics Anonymous is that the patient gets a sponsor, someone who is not a doctor or a therapist or a family member—or even a friend—to whom she can tell all of the dark and dirty secrets in complete confidence. I call my sponsor when I feel confused about something—my work, my marriage, my friends—or if I simply want to chat with someone who knows my challenges. He's the first person I turn to. He's not a therapist; he's someone who is still working on his own personal recovery. He doesn't give me specific answers or advice, necessarily, but he reminds me how to find the answers for myself. His perspective often sheds light on my own path. By the same token, I act as a sponsor myself, for a young man who is not a patient, just a community member who checks in with me so that I know he's doing okay.

You could call it a sort of grown-up buddy system, but it works. Sponsors have learned how to listen and engage in a commitment to help their fellow traveler in recovery.

Moderation Management and Last Call

There are newer organizations in certain communities and on college campuses that support members who have not yet stopped their drugging and drinking. Moderation Management (MM) and

Last Call are support groups that meet regularly and help members learn how to manage their lives, set goals, and cut back on their substance abuse. Many of the members of these groups move on to AA when they are ready to make the commitment to abstinence. Although I believe that people with addictive tendencies ultimately must abstain completely from drinking and doing drugs, these groups might help "bridge the gap" for those who know they have a problem and desire an intermediary step. The groups are usually free, so they are available to people who can't afford a private therapist. These groups also welcome family members and nonaddicts who are concerned or who are affected by someone else's behavior, as well as those who simply want to learn more about the issue.

Heart of Recovery

There is a burgeoning community based on Shambhala Buddhism that combines the principles of meditation with the 12 steps. Heart of Recovery has meetings in many major cities, and the format is different from other such meetings. Similar to other Buddhist recovery groups that are growing in popularity, this meeting begins with the practice of sitting meditation, followed by comments and sharing.

I encourage you to find a group in your community that helps you meet other people in your situation, that supports you in your efforts to take responsibility for your addiction, and that can offer a wide network of local resources to get help. "It takes a village" to support our loved ones in trouble, and it is amazing what you will discover once you attend a meeting and start making connections.

A Sober Communal House

A transitional or sober living environment can be extremely helpful for you when you are moving on into the outside world. This is not the same as a "halfway house," which is used by people just released from a prison or a detention center. Sober facilities vary in services, structure, dynamics, and capacity. Generally run by a live-in manager, a sober facility is a structured household that usually integrates drug testing, curfews, meetings, and probation periods. Ask a lot of questions when viewing or selecting the sober living facility. It is an excellent extension of treatment, because safety and sobriety are the priorities. These facilities are growing in number across the country, and the costs vary, depending on where they are located and how many amenities they provide. Many colleges across the country now provide dormitories that are sober houses.

When a patient leaves a rehab center, it is highly recommended that he or she have a sober coach or companion. Most relapses occur after rehab when a patient must go back home or to work and may not understand how to establish new patterns of behavior. Companions assist you in setting goals, scheduling AA meetings, exploring daily challenges and their ramifications, examining attitudes and everyday feelings, considering alternative solutions, and making healthier decisions. A sober companion or coach is not the same thing as an AA sponsor (the former is usually paid, for one thing), but he or she can fill a similar role for more hours in the day.

A sober community in any form is a vital component to help you achieve success in recovery. Many groups cost no money and ask no questions. If you cannot afford rehab or private therapy, go to one of these meetings as soon and as often as you can. You will feel immediate benefits and perhaps find all of the motivation and support you need.

Roger Ebert, Writing about AA

It is free and everywhere and has no hierarchy, and no one in charge. It consists of the people gathered in that room at that time, many perhaps unknown to one another. I have attended meetings in church basements, school rooms, a court room, a hospital, a jail, banks, beaches, living rooms, the back rooms of restaurants, and on board the *Queen Elizabeth II*. There's usually coffee. Sometimes someone brings cookies. We sit around, we hear the speaker, and then those who want to comment do. Nobody has to speak. Rules are, you don't interrupt anyone, and you don't look for arguments.... I came to love the program and the friends I was making through meetings, some of whom are close friends to this day. It was the best thing that ever happened to me.

What I hadn't expected was that AA was virtually theater. As we went around the room with our comments, I was able to see into lives I had never glimpsed before. I met people from every walk of life, and we all talked easily with one another because we were all there for the same reason, and that cut through the bullshit. One was Humble H., who was as funny as a stand-up comedian. I began to realize that I had tended to avoid some people because of my instant conclusions about who they were and what they would have to say. I discovered that everyone, speaking honestly and openly, had important things to tell me.

9

Working the
12 Steps

Those who attend Alcoholics Anonymous (AA) study the 12 steps of recovery and gain insight into methods that will help them maintain sobriety. This chapter gives you my take on the steps and also includes worksheets to help you sort things out, whether you are following the program or not. The beauty of AA is that you get to work out these issues with the guidance of a sponsor, who maintains your confidences. If you also brought these worksheets to a psychotherapist, they might help draw out issues that normally don't come to mind in your scheduled hour.

I highly recommend you think about these topics, whether or not you are going through the 12 steps at this time. It will prompt you to collect your thoughts about many issues in your life, even those not related to recovery.

These worksheets can be downloaded from the Hills website, www.thehillscenter.com, and you can write on the pages to your heart's content.

Step One

"We admitted we were powerless over alcohol/our addiction—that our lives had become unmanageable."

Here is where healing begins. We don't get anywhere until we've completed the first step in the recovery process. You might get through this step in your own personal and private way, but sometimes it helps to work on Step One in a more formal way. My personal opinion is, Whatever works for you. I know some of you may have gone through this step several times. If so, perhaps it's time to try a new way through it. Or, maybe you've been sober for a while and would like to go through the steps as a refresher.

Remember, your powerlessness is due to a disease, not a moral failure. Something inside us makes us want to drink and take drugs, makes us obsess about it. We have become compulsive and self-absorbed and pretty fucking miserable. We make our loved ones miserable, as well. Of course, we are often in denial at this point, too. It's "someone else's fault," right? Someone's expectations are just too high, so we get high. And it's shameful to admit we are messed up.

Starting Step One will be proactive in finding happiness again. Accept your situation with an open mind. You need to surrender, at this point, if you haven't already done so, due to arrest or injury. Maybe you don't think you need to do this at all, in which case you will probably change your mind before you finish this step. Of course, you need to stop drinking and using drugs before you achieve Step One. It may seem that all is lost right now, but you must get through this painful step to begin your journey. Don't confuse powerlessness with weakness. This simply means the driving force in your life is out of control. The thing that creates change is intense personal pain. The more emotion and pain you can work through will bring you closer to the psychic shift toward recovery.

It might help if you write down your thoughts, to arrive at answers to the following questions:

- When I am obsessing about using drugs or alcohol, my thought patterns focus on _____
- Usually, the consequences of this are _____
- I also behave compulsively when I _____
- My disease has affected me in these ways: _____
- I have been obsessing about _____
- I acted compulsively most recently when I _____
- Even though I know better, I have been telling myself and others that my behavior is due to _____
- I think my addiction isn't so bad because _____
- I have been avoiding taking steps because I am afraid I will learn _____
- The signs that I cannot ignore my disease any longer are _____
- I first suspected I had a problem when _____
- My reaction to the word *powerless* is _____
- When I first decided I was never going to drink or do drugs anymore, this is what happened: _____
- I have done extreme things to maintain my addiction to drugs or alcohol, such as _____
- When I am high and acting out, this is what I do: _____
  _____

- Signs that my life has become unmanageable are _____
  _____

- I have done certain things that are illegal as a result of my addiction or alcoholism, such as _____

- I have had these troubles with my family members and friends: _____

- I think of only myself and not about others when I _____
  _____

- I have ignored trouble signs about myself or my family or work when I _____

- When I get high, I am usually doing it to change my feelings about _____

- I believe that I can still control my addiction if I _____
  _____

- The one thing that I would never be able to do if I'm not high is _____

- I might be able to keep my addiction under control if I
  _____

- My reservations about giving up my addiction are _____
  _____

- I know I am an alcoholic or an addict, but _____

- If I agree that the only way to recovery is to "surrender" to it, then I will feel _____

- Since I no longer need to cover up my disease, then I can also finally be honest about _____

- I am willing to live my life differently in order to _____
  _____

- I will stop rejecting these things without trying to accept them first: _____

- In recovery meetings, I have trouble believing _____

- I am practicing being open-minded by _____

- I am going to give recovery an honest effort by _____ _____
- I accept who I am and can practice humility _____
- I am now starting to feel hopeful about _____
- I have made peace with the fact that _____
- Accepting my disease is necessary for continued recovery because _____
- I feel ready to move on to Step Two because _____

Step Two

"Came to believe that a Power greater than ourselves could restore us to sanity."

Okay, now that you've ditched your illusions, here's the good news: there is hope. The insanity and pain in your life can be eliminated! The second step will help you fill a void and realize you can be healed. Admitting that your prior life was "insane" might seem extreme, but the Big Book defines insanity as "repeating the same mistakes and expecting different results." Remember how many times you told yourself, "This time will be different"? After you've said this (and it failed to prove true) for ten or twenty years, that qualifies as "insane." This is when you notice sanity returning, because you start to make better choices in your life. You start to think before you act.

This step is not about religion. Remember, I am not a religious person, so I am here to remind you that Step Two is not about religion. Although the program is spiritual in nature, it works for people who are atheist, agnostic, Buddhist, Muslim, Christian, Jewish, pagan, Gaian, alien, Mayan, or doorknob. It is whatever works for you. As you know, I discovered my higher power working with a teenager in New York City, and I declared from that moment on that this was how I personally defined the higher power in the 12 steps. Our personal histories play a large role in the power we believe in, and rightly so. You can also take your time to define your higher power—you don't have to decide right now what that power will be.

Over time, you will choose your own power, preferably one that is loving and kind and that can help you stay sane and in recovery. Don't worry about who or what this power is. The group meetings are a good higher power in themselves, and so is the group of people within the meetings. As long as you understand that this power has the ability to restore you to sanity, and it is a power greater than you alone, it is a valid realization you can work with.

This is the step where you replace desperation with hope. If you're like me, you tried everything else before starting the 12 steps, and you may not be sure this will work, either. Yet while sitting in an AA meeting, you have met others who have the same disease that you have. You can trust them, because they've been where you've been, right? When you realize that they are staying clean and doing all right, you will start to feel hope. One day, during a meeting or after a meeting, this realization will knock you upside the head.

During the years to come, hope will be rejuvenated for you in this community. You will feel some painful moments, to be sure, but something hopeful will replace that pain. The pain will not be more than you can bear, and you will not go through it alone. Recovery, growth, change, and a greater sense of freedom are inevitable when you achieve this step. You will have no more secrets or isolation. Think about these topics as you work on Step Two:

- Today I feel hopeful about: _____
- I used to think I could control my drinking/drugging by

_____

- I can't believe my addiction made me do this: _____
- My disease made me I overreact when I _____
- My addictive insanity told me I could solve all my problems by _____
- The mistake I most often keep repeating is _____
- Here are things that are more powerful than I am: _____
_____
- My fears about believing in a higher power are _____
_____
- Stories about power that I have heard from others in recovery include _____
- I can help build my belief in power over time by _____
_____
- Here are signs that a power greater than me is working in my life: _____
- I need sanity right now in order to _____
- I need to stop doing these things in order to restore my sanity: _____
- Because sanity takes some time to achieve, here's what I will do when I get angry or frustrated in the meantime: _____
_____
- In sobriety, I notice that one thing I no longer get insane about is _____
- I know that I can't recover alone, so I will be open-minded today about receiving help by _____
- My life has changed so far in recovery, which can be seen by _____
- Here's a story I heard in a 12-step meeting that I have actually applied to my own life: _____
- I am now willing to do this, which I would never do before: _____
_____

- Here's an action I took or a decision I made that demonstrates my sense of faith in my recovery: _____
- These are the fears I have in trusting in my sobriety: _____
- Here's something I can do to prove my trust in a power greater than myself: _____
- I can seek help from my higher power by _____
- When I have had enough humility to seek help from my sponsor or at meetings, this is what has happened: _____
- Today, this is what I can do to help myself "come to believe": _____

Step Three

"Made a decision to turn our will and our lives over to the care of God *as we understood Him*."

In this step, "God as we understood Him" is the same thing as "higher power." Now, let's transform your sense of hope and trust into action. You may not understand the steps yet, and that's okay, but it's time to make a decision. You may not like making decisions all on your own, without the help of alcohol or drugs. Decisions require responsibility, and this is a big one, so it may take some time. You are not expected to make wholesale changes to your life all at once.

The third step suggests we turn our will and our lives over to the care of the God of our understanding. This means we will allow someone or something to care for us but not control us. This is a decision about changing direction, to stop fighting against the natural flow of events in our lives, to stop trying to control everything ourselves. After all, we haven't done such a great job. We are accepting that a power greater than ourselves will do it better. This is when you can explore what the word *God* means to you personally. Your understanding of "God" doesn't have to be certain or complete or even resemble any other person's definition. Maybe all you know is what God isn't. Our goal here is to start a search for the meaning as it pertains to you. This definition may grow and change with time, but for now, let's work with what we can.

If you hate making decisions, well, now's the time to learn how to face them head on. Turn your life over to the God of your understanding, which is something I decide to do every single day. It's a decision I make in my heart and spirit, if not always in my mind. It's internal and natural to me now.

Making a decision means nothing unless we take action to affirm it. In the past, we simply followed our impulses and acted selfishly in our pursuit of drugs and alcohol, remaining isolated. We forgot we had a conscience, let alone a higher power. This isn't about giving up on making personal goals. It's about starting to consider what our higher power intends for us, starting with sobriety. Our concept of this power may change over time, especially if we feel the need for more caring.

Also, you might find success in first turning over your destructive self-will. Not just your addiction, but your will. Then, gradually or quickly, you will turn over your life to that higher power. Your family, your finances, your work, your friendships, your children, your health—you must let it all go. The action you need to take may simply be making the declaration that you will turn over your will and your life to your higher power or will go to a meeting or will reach out to your sponsor. You often feel more willing after you experience the deepest despair. Use that pain to your advantage, and take action to commit to a higher power.

Hope is born when you start to see that life is full of possibilities. It can be a thrill when you begin to believe that you can truly achieve your heart's desire. This builds faith and gives you courage to take more steps toward fulfillment. When you apply that faith, you start to build trust. Sometimes you have to "turn it over" repeatedly, and remind yourself every day of this mantra, even when you're having a lousy day. But it will give you freedom. Write down your thoughts to finish these sentences:

- I have acted on my self-will, excluding thought of all others, when I _____
- This is what makes me feel peaceful and makes it easier for me to remain _____
- My fears about making this decision, even just for today, are _____
- The areas of my life I have trouble "turning over" are

  _____
- The action I will take today to follow through with my decision is _____
- If I pursue what I want, how will my goals hurt myself or anyone else? _____
- My own will was not enough to guide me, which proved true when _____
- When things are going well in recovery, I sometimes forget that it is from God's will and not my own, such as when

  _____
- I feel uncomfortable about the word or concept of "God" because _____
- Today, my understanding of a power greater than myself is

  _____
- I will try to communicate with my higher power today by

  _____
- This is how I feel about the God of my understanding:

  _____

- It is difficult to believe in any sort of God when things like this happen: _____
- I may not understand the higher power, but I will ask for acceptance and strength about _____
- My higher power has helped me confront fears and frustrations when _____
- My current higher power is not working as it should, so I will change it by _____
- My life will change when I turn it over to my higher power by _____
- I have trusted my higher power to care for my life when

  _____
- When I think about surrender and willingness, I _____

  _____
- I reinforce my decision to allow my higher power to care for my life when I _____
- I am willing to let recovery prevail in my life, and I can show it by _____
- To me, hope means _____
- To me, faith means _____
- To me, trust means _____
- I have seen proof of positive action when I _____

  _____
- Here is the evidence that I am confident in recovery:

  _____
- Recently, I demonstrated my commitment to recovery by

  _____
- My lingering reservations about turning over my will and my life to a higher power are _____
- I feel more courage now to do this: _____

  _____

Step Four

"Made a searching and fearless moral inventory of ourselves."

The reason you drink or use drugs is that you feel you are a "victim." A victim of your parents, the courts, your boss, your girlfriend, your husband, whoever. You are drowning in self-pity. Yet there is no power in being a victim. The fourth step is about taking personal responsibility for your behavior, looking at your own role in this situation. This step shows you how to begin to find out who you are, how you can like yourself, and how you really can reach happiness and serenity, if you stop being a victim and empower yourself to change. Steps Four through Nine are the ones you will repeat over and over again in the years to come. Every time you do Step Four, you will discover more and deeper insights into who you are, as you get closer to that healthy core inside yourself. You might see another way that you've caused someone harm or another form of denial or addiction.

As you learn more about yourself, this step will bring you closer to a sort of spiritual awakening. This step is where you identify exactly what you did wrong, for the purpose of finding true freedom. You felt isolated, depressed, and confused long before you started drinking and drugging. Taking this sort of inventory lists all of the sources of your pain and personal conflicts and expunges them so that they no longer have any hold over your actions.

"Searching and fearless" are sweeping and ambitious words. You have to be fearless because it takes courage to be honest, even when you'd just as soon forget some of your most shameful transgressions. You have to make a seemingly endless list, even when you're tired of thinking about things you did wrong. You have to maintain faith in the process and trust your higher power to guide you through it. This step is one of the most difficult, because it requires a lot of work. Take your time. Do a little at a time. But do a little every day or every other day. Don't put it down for long. It is easy to avoid this, but give yourself permission to feel fear.

The word *moral* here refers to your own morals—not society's morals or someone else's code. It's your personal code. They are your personal values and principles. Many times, your resentments or fears are related to other people or an organization. Feel free to write whatever you need, but remember to bring it back to your role in the situation. Ask your sponsor for help.

Your inventories might reveal bad behavior patterns that need adjusting, a need to end relationships or let go of old resentments and anger. Most of us are afraid of change, even if it's ultimately for our own good. We're afraid to think about some things we've done in the past. We're afraid to learn just how much our addictions hurt us and others. We're afraid of more pain. We are afraid even to let go of fear.

Remember to incorporate the first three steps into this one: willingness, honesty, faith, and trust. Get a notebook or a computer or whatever you're comfortable with using to make a list. A long list! Find a private place, and ask your higher power for the ability to be searching and fearless. Write down old feelings that you can't forget or forgive, and think about the ways in which you set yourself up to be disappointed and hurt. Take breaks and talk with your sponsor throughout this step. These lists help you identify patterns of destructive behavior and will help release you from cycles of anger and self-destruction.

In addition to actually writing down your inventory, separately from this, think about these things while you work the fourth step. Some of these issues may not apply to you, but most of them do, in one way or another.

- My fears about working this step are _____
- Being searching and fearless, for me, means _____
- I can handle this inventory because I discussed it with _____
- The values and principles important to me are _____ _____
- I resent the following people: _____
- The reasons are _____
- I resent these schools, employers, churches, or groups: _____
- The reasons are _____
- I acted the way I did because _____
- I developed resentments because I didn't want to believe _____
- My own role in causing these resentments was _____ _____
- My resentments have affected my relationships with ____ _____
- The recurring themes in my list of resentments are ____ _____
- I have the most trouble letting myself feel _____ _____
- I covered up how I really felt by _____
- I shut down my feelings because _____
- My feelings are triggered when I think about _____ _____
- I acted the way I did in those situations because I _____ _____
- Now that I have identified these feelings, I will _____ _____

- I feel guilty or ashamed about _____
- Things I did that make me feel guilty or ashamed include _____
- I acted that way because I believed _____
- I am afraid I'll be hurt when _____
- I'm afraid I will lose _____
- I am afraid of _____
- I have disguised my fear by _____
- The thing I fear most about exposing _____
- If I reveal this, I am afraid this will happen: _____
- My fear of being hurt has affected my relationships _____
- I compulsively seek relationships by _____
- The repeating dynamic for my family is _____
- I have avoided intimacy or commitment with partners and friends by _____
- I hurt someone because I was afraid he/she would hurt me first, when I _____
- In my relationships, I consider others' feelings as _____
- I set myself up as a victim when I was in a relationship with _____
- The patterns I see regarding my relationships with friends and neighbors are _____
- The patterns I see regarding my relationships with coworkers are _____
- I have had problems at work when _____
- My school friends make (or made) me feel _____

- My feelings about people in authority are _____
- I am a member of certain organizations, including _____
  _____

- Sometimes my expectations in relationships are not ful-filled because _____
- I feel shy sometimes because early experiences with trust and intimacy _____
- I ended a relationship that could have been salvaged when
  _____

- I am different person when I'm around _____
- I overcompensate by _____
- The most damaging aspects of my relationships are
  _____

- I can have healthier relationships if I _____
- My relationship with my higher power is _____
- I confused love with sex when I _____
- I used sex to avoid loneliness when I _____
- I am ashamed of my sexual behavior when I remember
  _____

- I am comfortable with my sexuality because _____
  _____

- I am comfortable with other people's sexuality, except
  _____

- To me, a healthy relationship means _____
- I was abused, when _____
- This is how I feel about the abuse: _____
- I will take these steps to ask my higher power for help and to restore myself to wholeness: _____
- I feel ashamed about the time I abused someone, when I
  _____

- Right before I was abusive, I was thinking or feeling

  _____

- I will get through the painful aspects of this step by

  _____

- My best qualities are, in my opinion, _____
- Other people tell me that I am good at _____
- I show concern for others when I _____
- I practice my spiritual life when I _____
- My relationship with my sponsor is _____
- I have accomplished these goals: _____
- I am planning to reach these goals: _____
- I show my gratitude for my recovery when I _____

  _____

- I am committed to living by these values: _____

  _____

- Something that is hard for me to admit to in my inventory
  is _____
- I have not yet admitted to this secret: _____
- One story I frequently tell that is not really true is _____

  _____

Step Five

"Admitted to God, to ourselves, and to another
human being the exact nature of our wrongs."

After Step Four, you should feel some sense of relief, but the
hard part is not finished yet. Now you need to admit the nature
of your wrongs—to God, to yourself, and to another person—by
revealing the inventory from Step Four. You will feel more fear,
perhaps, that you will be judged or rejected. Reading this list out
loud to someone is not easy because it might stir up old feelings

from the past, may make them all seem too real. Yet by now you should see that others in recovery have survived this step. Others in recovery who have healthy relationships with friends and family gained the most benefits from Step Five.

This step will move you toward real change, whether you think you want it or not. You know you need to change. You will gain in courage and trust through this step, by working through your fears and making admissions. Ask your higher power for courage. Share your concerns with your sponsors or members of your recovery group. Move forward, despite your fears.

You may not understand the exact nature of your failings until you are finished with this step. Making your admission to another person will help you understand your failings. For most of us, that person is our sponsor. He or she will help you understand what you are truly responsible for and also what you are not responsible for. Your sponsor might also share with you from his or her own inventory, and you will learn that you are not unique. Of course, you may also choose someone else whom you trust, but your sponsor understands the process and may provide the greatest insight, without judgment. This step helps you be honest with yourself and develop further trust in someone else. Some of it will be painful, and you will want to shut down and not listen to what your sponsor says. Remember, though, that caving in to fear has not helped you in the past. Be courageous, because completing this step will change the course of your life. You were not great at commitment when you were drinking and drugging. This step will prove that you can stay committed.

Consider these topics:

- The fears I have at this point are _____
- The first four steps prepared me for this by _____
_____

- I admitted my addiction when I started the First Step. Now I admit to my innermost self that _____
- This admission will change the direction of my life by

  _____

- I feel confident about whom I will admit these to, because that person is _____
- I will learn more about my inventory when I share it because _____
- I observe certain patterns in my behavior, such as _____

  _____

- The exact nature of my wrongs differs from my actions, in that _____
- This practice of trust makes me feel _____
- The fifth step will make my life better because _____

  _____

- I will work up the courage for this step by _____
- The time and place for admitting to another person is scheduled for _____
- Without using alcohol and drugs, I sense my feelings are different because _____
- I am a good person, right at this moment, because _____
- I am a good person now, in spite of _____
- After sharing my inventory, I feel a sense of _____
- After the fifth step, my relationship with my higher power

  _____

- My view of myself has changed _____ _____
- This step has exhausted me, but now I feel ready to

  _____

Step Six

"Were entirely ready to have God remove all these defects of character."

By now, you should be developing a stronger sense of hope, and you're probably feeling somewhat humble—"humility" means you are able to see yourself more clearly. You've learned how the defects in your character have harmed you and other people. You have identified patterns in your behavior that compensate for your defects. This step enables you to eliminate your defects, and you may feel motivated to plow right through.

As with other steps, however, this one takes a while. You may be impatient to remove these defects, but you still need to be ready. This step requires you to study just how this will happen. If only a higher power can remove these defects, then what role can you play in the process? You still must confront your fear of change and step into the unknown once these defects are gone. Some of these defects are things you considered "survival skills," after all. What if you lose your job or turn into a boring person? What if there is nothing left after all of your defects have been removed? These are normal thoughts during this step. No one is perfect. Writing your thoughts on these topics will help you with this step:

- Some of my defects are things I sort of like about myself, such as _____
- The parts of me that will be removed are _____
- I have been through the sixth step before, and I find this defect is still with me: _____
- I believe this defect can be removed by _____
- I have changed already in these other ways: _____
- In stressful situations, I will avoid my defects by _____
- I will get help dealing with my recurring defects by _____

- When I try to control my defects myself, the results are

  _____

- Instead of suppressing my defects, I will have my higher power remove them by _____ _____
- I can take action to show that I am ready by _____
- I will not analyze my defects but will raise my awareness of them by _____
- I will find love not by using my defects but by _____
- When I practice one of my character defects, it is because I am feeling _____
- I can live without this defect by instead doing _____
- When I slip back into a character defect, I won't despair. I will _____
- Today I showed my commitment to recovery by _____
- Today I am willing to be honest, even when I _____
- I am not ready to have my character defects removed today

  _____

- I will get out of my own way to let the higher power in, when I _____
- I am still afraid that _____
- I will not be too critical with myself about _____ _____
- I have increased my trust in God by _____
- Today I am proud of myself for _____
- I wish I were more _____
- I would like to think about others more, so I will _____

  _____

- When I can stop worrying about all of the lies I have told in the past, I will spend more time on _____ _____
- I now see myself in the future as doing these things: _____

  _____

Step Seven

"Humbly asked Him to remove our shortcomings."

It probably seems as if the 12 steps do a lot of overlapping, but there are reasons for this blended process. In Step Six, you were ready for the removal of character defects; in Step Seven, you will become spiritually prepared to ask your higher power to remove them. Part of the preparation means learning what "humbly" means. You also have to learn how to replace the character defects with spiritual principles.

Humility serves a purpose in your life. Please remember that it bears no relation to humiliation or worthlessness. Humility is your humanity. Humility is the healthy part of you that is left after you strip away the traits of addiction: denial, ego, manipulation, lies, and games. You have learned how well you can control your own life, in sobriety. Perhaps you now recognize that kindness is not the same thing as weakness. By now, you've realized that it's totally acceptable for you to show your feelings. You started these steps feeling misunderstood, self-pity, and defensiveness, but now you see how you actually created your own misery yourself. You have wasted many opportunities and made some bad choices.

With humility, you allow yourself to feel some compassion for yourself. You're not perfect. No one is. Even normal people make bad decisions once in a while. You're doing your very best now. You are making connections with other people and admitting your failings.

There are many ways to think of your higher power, including as God. I consider these words interchangeable, so do not be alarmed by my reference to God. It is what you believe it is, regardless of what it is called. By the same token, the ritual you use to communicate with your higher power is often referred to as "prayer." You may call it whatever you like, but it is helpful to learn to understand "prayer" when it is used in this context. Ask others in recovery how they "pray" to their higher powers. Do not attempt to remove your shortcomings on your own; it won't work.

You will make this request of your higher power more than once. In fact, you will ask it repeatedly, for the rest of your life. It's not a hard thing to do. Then, get out of the way. It will take some time to see the results of this step, but stay out of your own way.

- The healthy parts of myself that I now recognize are _____

  _____

- Humility affects my recovery by _____
- My relationship with the God of my understanding is now

  _____

- My higher power can do more for me than simply help me stay sober. My higher power can _____
- My ritual for communicating with my higher power—my act of "prayer"—is _____
- I will ask my higher power to remove my shortcomings by

  _____

- I will invite my higher power to work in my life by _____

  _____

- I will maintain awareness of my higher power by remembering to _____
- Knowing that my higher power is caring for me makes me feel _____
- I have accepted my powerlessness over my addictions, as well as over my _____
- My feelings about surrender now are _____
- In order to avoid impatience with this step, I will _____
- I recently took advantage of an opportunity for growth when I _____

- I will avoid thinking of myself as too powerful by _____
- I feel I have become a better person because _____
  _____
- I feel I am a different person since I started the steps because _____
- The shortcomings that have been removed or lessened in my life are _____
- My life feels more spiritual because _____
- To nourish my spiritual life, I _____

Step Eight

"Made a list of all persons we had harmed, and became willing to make amends to them all."

Now that you have started to repair yourself and develop a relationship with your higher power, it is time to bring other people into your healing. These are people you love, people you don't love, people you don't even see anymore, people you harmed on purpose or by accident, old friends and family, and new friends as well. This is about identifying damage that you may have caused— not figuring out why you hurt someone or whether you intended to cause hurt; just identifying that you hurt someone, period. It is possible that damage you caused to others is beyond repair or that you were not actually responsible, even though you believe you are. Simply identify the injury and who it affected, and decide whether you are now willing to make amends. Many of these situations might be the same ones you identified in previous steps, but this is a new angle from which to work through them.

This step does not require you to make the amends, only to become willing to do so. It is enough, in this step, to make a list of people, including those to whom you may have already made amends. Many family members and coworkers are probably already pleased that you have stopped drinking or using drugs, so that damage may already be in repair. Yet this isn't really about being willing to apologize. This step is about being willing to change. Conversations with people you have hurt are a powerful means of spiritual growth for you, as much as they might also comfort others. This step is about letting you feel equal to other people, instead of feeling inferior or shameful. You will address your responsibilities, and then you will be free.

Discuss this step with your sponsor (as with all steps), who will help you identify what was harmful in your past. Some harmful behaviors are more subtle than others, of course. Maybe you're not even sure whether you caused harm to anyone or exactly what kind of harm you may have caused. If you are unsure, include that person on your list anyway, because you might recall the details later. Sometimes you did something harmful but are not sure who exactly was harmed by it. If as a student you cheated on a test, you harmed other students and your teacher, as well as yourself, so you all belong on the list. Losing an old friendship, even though you're not sure why it happened: this belongs on your list. Include people who offered to help you, but you rebuffed them. Add to your list the people you railed at in the rehab center.

This is not about running around apologizing to everyone you know. Your sponsor will help you consider what to do about confessing "too much" to your loved ones. Sometimes confirming a marital infidelity or a criminal activity will only cause further harm, which is not the goal. In addition, some of these people also harmed you. This is the step where you must set aside blame and resentment. This step helps you reach forgiveness, for them and for yourself.

You might be tempted to avoid this step, because you may not want to talk to some of these people. Write down as many names as you can remember. Your sponsor will help you decide on the best approach for each one. He or she will also provide support and encouragement. It may help to think about the following:

- I will slow down and discuss with my sponsor whether I should make amends for _____
- I feel resentful about making amends for _____
- I will make amends for the harm I caused myself by _____
  _____

- I am willing to make amends now because I have faith that
  _____

- I am less willing to make amends about _____
- I will pay the money I owe to _____
- I will forgive and make amends even for _____
- My experience with honesty in the previous steps has shown me that I can _____
- It is important to accept responsibility for the harm I caused because _____
- The higher power will give me these things to help me become willing to make amends: _____
- I am afraid that _____
- These are the names I wasn't willing to put on the list at first, but now I will: _____
- Today I observed a character defect in someone else, and I felt _____
- I am feeling more connected to _____
- I feel more compassion and empathy for _____
  _____

Step Nine

"Made direct amends to such people wherever possible, except when to do so would injure them or others."

This step would simply not be possible until you have completed the first eight. How on earth could you possibly sit down with all of the people you've hurt, unless you were this well prepared? But you are ready now: you have a relationship with a higher power, you understand your personal responsibility, and you have developed humility and willingness. Now you should strengthen your self-awareness and sense of forgiveness, because you will need them throughout this step.

Step Nine is not achieved in a specific time period. Many of you will complete it, or you might continue making amends for years. You will also spend years making even more amends to your loved ones, simply by practicing your newly acquired spiritual principles. Even after you pay off your debts, you have other "debts" to consider, such as personal favors from friends and coworkers and avoiding future debts. This list may never end, and that's okay.

If you've done Step Nine before, you might feel a little hesitant, remembering what you went through the last time you did this. Most of you probably had some positive experiences with this step already, but not everyone you've hurt has a positive reaction and offers you instant forgiveness. However, it is not your job to predict how you will be received. It is merely an opportunity to repair what you damaged in the course of your disease, so that you can lay old problems to rest. If someone you hurt also hurt you, you are not making amends for both of you— only for your part. Asking forgiveness also requires acts of forgiveness on your part. It's about resolution, restoration, and restitution.

Working with your sponsor will help you stay focused and help you decide whether to make amends face-to-face with someone or in some other way. Your sponsor will help you determine whether some amends will cause more harm than good and should not be made. You might also seek legal counsel, if you have committed a crime, and weigh such effects on your loved ones. Some people to whom you owe amends may have long passed away, in which case you might contact their children or make a donation to an appropriate charity. Each situation in your life is different, and your conversations will guide you in understanding what to do, either directly or indirectly.

Of course, you have a huge amount of fear that the damage cannot be repaired, and, in some cases, it may not be. But you will free yourself of the burdens, and this process will change you for the better, despite the painful moments. You will start to feel lighter, freer, and maybe even ecstatic that you are able to heal some old hurts. You have proved your humility and your commitment to a better life.

- Humility helps me in this step by _____
- Making amends, to me, means _____
- Making amends is a further commitment to change because _____
- I am preparing for this step by _____
- I am looking forward to making amends to _____
  _____
- I am fearful about making amends to _____
- I have faith that I can pay off financial amends because
  _____
- My expectations about making amends are _____
- If my amends are not well received by someone, I will
  _____

- Some of the names on my amends list are complicated situations because _____
- Amends I make that could have very serious consequences are _____
- I owe amends to someone who has passed away, so I will think of a unique way to make amends for that by _____ _____
- When I can't find someone on my amends list, I will _____ _____
- When someone tells me that he or she cannot or will not forgive me, I will _____
- I feel much lighter after making amends to _____ _____
- I felt the effects of someone's feelings other than my own when I made amends to _____
- I am having trouble finding forgiveness for _____
- I will wait a longer time to make amends to _____
- I realize now that I played a role in my own misery when I felt hurt by _____
- I can see now how I was hurt inadvertently by someone else who had problems when _____ _____
- I know my higher power forgives my actions because _____
- I felt pretty awful after I made amends to _____
- I won't lose hope if I receive a bad reaction because _____ _____
- I feel my freedom growing with this step, because _____ _____
- I will follow through with certain amends, such as _____ _____

- Remembering what I did will prevent me from ever doing this again: _____
- I feel less angry and more forgiving about _____
- Instead of carrying around guilt and resentment, I will start to do this more: _____
- I will further make amends to myself by planning to _____
- I felt the hurt when I heard this while making amends to someone: _____
- I didn't realize how much hurt I had caused when I _____
- I feel more love now because _____
- I give to myself now, and to others, when I _____
- I am less judgmental of others because _____
- I realize I trust more people now because I _____
- I forgive myself for _____
- I feel less obsessed now about _____
- Making amends to others makes me feel _____
- Step Nine has taught me that _____
- I can share this story with others as a good example of Step Nine: _____

Step Ten

"Continued to take personal inventory and when we were wrong promptly admitted it."

By now, you are probably feeling different. Maybe you feel less angry, more honest, more concerned about others, but these changes are not guaranteed to stay with you. You have to be vigilant and continue to ask yourself how you react to things, how much faith you still feel. You are probably more aware of how your actions affect others, and perhaps you pay more attention to how other people react to you. If you sense you've done something that hurt someone, now you may feel a natural instinct to step up and admit your mistakes right away.

You might need to focus on certain difficulties, and this step will help you identify them. As you continue to take a personal inventory, you may confront new challenges that arise during your recovery. You are simply more aware of everything you do and see. You assess your feelings and tie them to particular events or actions. Perhaps you feel crappy, even though you are doing pretty well overall. Maybe you're avoiding some difficult steps or indulging in some old behavior. Maybe you feel angry about something, and you are doing your best to suppress it, because you know it's not a good feeling. You still have a right to get angry about something or sad or confused; don't ignore this feeling. Take a positive action to remedy it, or get out of the situation entirely. Or, instead of suppressing a negative feeling, see if you can simply let the feeling go.

Points of confusion may be clarified and remedied by conversations with your sponsor. The goal here is simply to stay aware, to stay balanced, to focus on positive things, instead of negative ones, and not to be hard on yourself. This ritual will become second nature to you, over time. You won't sit down and make a list every day, but you will pay attention, which will make you feel better.

- I am confused about my feelings and my actions when

  _____

- I recently admitted I was wrong when _____

- I am trying to be less rigid in my new attitude by _____

  _____

- I am less demanding of others when I _____

- When someone says something hurtful to me, I _____
  _____

- I made a mistake when _____
- When I am wrong, it affects _____
- I can't identify what I did wrong when _____
- It's hard not to blame the other person for my wrong when
  _____

- I have accumulated new wrongs recently, such as _____
  _____

- But I am grateful for _____
- I made the problem worse when I talked immediately to
  _____

- When I promptly admit my wrongs, I change my behavior
  by _____
- When I take my personal inventory, I notice positive things,
  too, such as _____
- I stopped insisting I was right when _____
- My new life in recovery is _____
- I feel uncomfortable about acknowledging that I now do
  this well: _____
- Today I took a personal inventory and _____
- I will correct or maintain this by _____
- Today I reaffirmed my faith in my higher power when I
  _____

- I was of service to other people today when I _____
  _____

- I saw some old patterns in my life today, and I _____
- I felt fear about _____
- I am taking myself less seriously about _____
- Today I am feeling _____

- I am willing to change because _____
- Today I wish I had _____
- I felt conflict when _____
- I owe amends to _____
- I would have done this differently: _____
- I will remember to do this again: _____
- Today I talked about my recovery with _____
- I feel good about _____
- I did not take my usual "easy way out" today when _____
  _____
- I was tired today, but still I _____
- The last time I went to a meeting _____
- My self-honesty is helping me _____
- I am amazed at how honest I am about _____
- It is hard for me to maintain integrity when _____
  _____
- I change the subject when _____
- I felt bad about my reaction when _____
- The tenth step has helped my relationships by _____
  _____
- I feel a sense of community with _____
- It feels natural to admit my wrongs, because _____
  _____
- I feel as valuable as anyone else now, because _____
  _____
- I act differently now when I _____
- I live in the present more easily now, because _____
  _____
- I feel more harmony when _____
- I have found more meaning and purpose _____

Step Eleven

"Sought through prayer and meditation to
improve our conscious contact with God *as
we understood Him*, praying only for knowledge
of His will for us and the power to carry that out."

"God as we understood Him": remember, that's your higher power, no matter what you call him or her or it. This higher power, this God as you understand Him, is an entity with which you have already made a conscious contact. You developed awareness of, and learned to trust, your higher power in earlier steps. You called on this entity to help you through some difficult stages. This step teaches you to reach out to that entity, in what is referred to as prayer and meditation. If you don't like those words, please find a way to work around them, or call these communications whatever you prefer. But prayer and meditation are what will strengthen your connection to this higher power and keep you on a spiritual path of great fulfillment. Members of AA refer to "prayer" when they mean talking to your higher power and to "meditation" when listening to your higher power.

Your path is uniquely your own and always will be. It depends on what religion or traditions you practice, where you live, what you do, and what you believe. Because you have changed a great deal in the course of your recovery, you may need to make adjustments for a changing spiritual life as well. It is an enjoyable experience, to explore your spiritual path. If you find something you don't like or can't accept, then move along down a different path. You will encounter new people and new ideas and possibly be astounded by things you learn. No matter how long you have lived in a particular religious or cultural setting, the steps in recovery will cause a shift in spirituality, and you should be flexible about following where it leads. You will learn new things about yourself along the way, and that may be the most amazing part of it all.

Remember, spirituality is not the same as religion. This is about spiritual principles and relying on a power greater than ourselves, whether that power is God, Allah, Mother Nature, or an AA group. Discovering your spiritual path is up to you, and it can't always be found in religious institutions. That is why this is always a new journey in recovery. Talk with people, read books, discuss this with your sponsor. Your path will come into focus, even if you change course a few times. There is no hurry. Enjoy the journey, and one day your higher power will knock you on the head, clear as day.

- My ideas about a higher power/God have been changing _____

- I feel the presence of my higher power when _____ _____

- I now understand about my higher power that _____ _____

- My higher power is _____
- I have felt the transformative power of this God when _____

- The spiritual path of my childhood was _____ _____
- Now my spiritual path is _____ _____
- I feel that my higher power cares for me because _____ _____

- I now have an open mind about _____
- I am going to try new paths of spirituality, such as _____ _____

- My path is _____
- I explore my spirituality when I _____
- I have confidence in my path, even though I'm not sure where it will lead, because _____
- My spiritual journey helps my recovery by _____

- I encourage the spiritual exploration of others, even if I don't understand it, because _____
- I maintain contact with my group members, even if my spiritual path is different, because _____
- My spirituality has helped me in fellowship with others by _____
- Even with my higher power, I need my group meetings in order to _____
- When I work with newcomers, I advise them about their higher powers by saying _____
- My spiritual path has contributed to my recovery by _____
- The forms of prayer that I use are _____
- In my prayers, I ask God to help me _____
- When I pray, I feel _____
- Praying helps me put in perspective things such as _____
- In moments of silence, I _____
- Prayers at group meetings make me feel _____
- I quiet my mind by _____
- I am open to meditation when _____
- After meditation, I feel that my decisions are _____
- Meditation has helped me _____
- I am conscious of my higher power when _____
- I see how the higher power works in my life when _____
- In hard times, my higher power _____
- I work to improve my contact with my higher power by _____

- God's will for me is not _____
- I go along with the will of my higher power when I _____ _____
- When I set goals, I let in my higher power so that _____ _____
- If I am honest about who I am, then my higher power _____
- I know I am living God's will for me when _____ _____
- I think that God's will for me _____
- I feel I have the power to carry out God's will when _____ _____
- Being assertive is okay when _____
- It is good to be cautious when _____
- I have a sense of humor about the times God shows me _____
- I have a commitment to prayer and meditation _____
- I feel most comfortable when I pray _____
- I am sometimes confused about _____
- I feel peace of mind when _____
- Today I meditated and _____
- I once prayed for and then regretted it when _____
- Some of my family members seem to wish that my recovery _____
- These things have changed in my life since I started my spiritual journey: _____
- The choices I make now are _____
- I defend my faith when _____
- I am no longer afraid of _____

- I have received from my higher power _____
- When I listen to other people now, I _____
- I look at my addiction now as _____

Step Twelve

"Having had a spiritual awakening as a result of these Steps, we tried to carry this message to alcoholics/addicts, and to practice these principles in all our affairs."

Your personal spiritual awakening is unlike anyone else's. Yet in your group meetings, you may hear others talk about having similar reactions: feeling free, caring more about other people, and participating in life more fully. To other people, your enlightenment may seem unbelievable. Your friends and family tell you that you seem like another person. You remember where you started from, and even you barely recognize your old self. This change took a lot of time. Indeed, you are still on the path of spiritual awakening and always on the road in recovery. You have slowly built a relationship with a higher power, which provides inspiration for further growth.

One day, when you work the steps all over again, you will have a different experience. You will then recognize meaning in actions that you didn't see before. But having completed the steps for the first time is a tremendous achievement. You are more honest now, more willing, and your spiritual awakening continues to grow. You may not even think about drinking or using drugs anymore. Can you even believe it? It was one miracle to stay clean and sober, and then, on top of that, you gained self-respect, made new friends, helped other people, and paid old debts. Along the way, someone somewhere gave you a reason to believe it could happen. Maybe it was a stranger at a meeting, your sponsor, the love of your family, or your higher power.

You will still encounter challenges in life. You may lose faith when bad things happen, but it will come back. You will receive messages of motivation when you need them, if you hang in and remain open to them. You can stay in recovery as long as you have hope. Now, you should carry that message, the one that saved you, by sharing it with others who need it. "We can only keep what we have by giving it away." Go to meetings, take on a service position, or become a sponsor for a new member. Sharing your message might become a challenge, because certain people aren't always ready to listen.

- My spiritual awakening is _____
- I have seen lasting changes in myself, such as _____

  _____
- I feel fellowship when I _____
- I carry this message to others who need it by _____

  _____
- I am sponsoring someone but _____
- I will carry the message another way when I fail, such as

  _____
- I get my ego out of the way when I _____
- When I see another addict or alcoholic behaving destructively, I _____
- I remain available when I _____
- Something I heard early in recovery that didn't make sense to me until much later was _____
- Even if I have had a terrible day, there's a positive message to carry, such as _____
- I go to my group meetings regularly because _____

  _____

- Other group members, like me, are _____
- I feel accepted because _____
- I connect with other recovering addicts and alcoholics because _____
- One example of another person's story that helped me is _____
- I practice the principles of recovery when I _____
- I practice compassion when I _____
- When someone I know relapses, I _____
- I give others the benefit of the doubt, such as _____
- When I feel an old urge to control a situation, instead I switch to trust and then _____
- When I start to feel self-righteous, I switch to a principle of humility by _____
- I find it difficult to practice the principles when _____
- I need to spend more time working on _____
- I feel that unconditional love is _____
- I will carry the message when _____
- When I perform selfless service, I feel _____
- When I have a setback, the principle of steadfastness _____
- Today I am grateful for _____
- I plan to revisit Step One when _____
- I feel good about _____
- Now I feel as if I can do something I couldn't do before, such as _____
- I will express my gratitude by _____

10

The Reality of Relapse

Robert Downey Jr. once said, "Stopping isn't hard. Not starting again is." Relapse is part of recovery. The movie columnist Roger Ebert, who has been sober for thirty years, said, "Since my surgery in July 2006, I have literally not been able to drink at all. Unless I go insane and start pouring booze into my g-tube, I believe I'm reasonably safe." Many studies show that more than half of those recovering from alcoholism or addiction will relapse at least once. Professional therapists expect relapse—the challenge in addiction is not so much quitting, but staying sober.

The one major problem with relapse is this: you may not get through it alive. Not long ago, one of my patients died when he relapsed with crack cocaine. He had relapsed before, and this time, his heart just gave out. Victor was thirty-eight years old and left behind a five-year-old son. I was one of the lucky ones after my own relapse: I survived.

I'd spent a year in rehab at age twenty and emerged clean and sober. I was finally somewhat independent and clear-headed. I made new friends and rented my own apartment. I didn't realize that I was still somewhat unfulfilled. I was mystified that my friends could have a drink now and then, with no ill effects. When we are sober and feeling okay, we often forget that we are addicts. We think we have recovered, that our "problem" has been cured. I rationalized that I could have a beer once in a while. Remember, addicts are good at manipulation, and, in this case, I was manipulating myself. I rationalized every step of the way: that I could drink socially, that I could take a pill sometimes, that I could smoke an occasional joint. During the course of four years after rehab, my beast slowly took control. I eventually got hooked back on cocaine and then said, "Fuck it," and went back on heroin. My relapse lasted twelve years. Twelve years! I don't know why I am still alive, except perhaps to prove that you, too, can start over again after a relapse.

Relapse is not a sign of weakness. It is part of the process. Sometimes just once is all it takes to show an addict that he or she is not in control. Sometimes, it happens more than once. Relapse begins when we get restless. We stop focusing on our inner selves and start focusing outward, blaming others for our situation, and perhaps getting angry that we have this condition. We begin to isolate ourselves, even if we're in therapy. Our negative thinking increases, and we start to believe that we don't need to be in recovery. As if to prove we are correct or in reaction to a small problem we are prowling for, we rationalize that we can have a drink. That we have the "right" to do whatever we want. This is basically purchasing a first-class return ticket for your disease, which convinces us that this time we can maintain control. This negative thinking is a certain route to relapse. We need to relearn how to stop thinking this way.

Don't be ashamed if you relapse, and don't judge those who relapse. I have a friend who, when he first started in AA, was crushed to learn that one of the group had relapsed.

"It felt like a betrayal," he said. It's not a betrayal. It is part of recovery. Peace is just around the corner. The longer you can prevent relapse, the sooner peace will arrive. We will simply step forward again and start the sobriety clock back at zero. Turn a negative into a positive. Yet remember: relapse can kill you. Be thankful you're alive. I know a lot of people who didn't survive the relapse and died.

Long after we stop drinking or using drugs, our formerly addicted brains still make us want to use them. Although we learn how to manage this craving, it can be triggered pretty easily: every time you see someone else have a drink, perhaps, or you hear a certain song on the radio or smell the whiff of pot at a concert. A porn addict might feel the trigger when he sees a computer screen. If we give in, that means the disease is still at work, and thus begins another self-destructive cycle of shame and guilt. Remember, our days when we were addicts were quite mundane and pointless: we spent most of our time planning to obtain drugs or alcohol and getting high and then got up the next day to do it all over again. Now we have a lot of extra time to fill, since we left the demons behind.

A patient on the verge of relapse may begin by feeling signs of anxiety, withdrawing from sober companions, feeling depressed, eating too much, and having an increased temptation to use, or a craving for, alcohol or drugs. A primary objective in recovery is to avoid the people who are your former party friends. This can be tough if there are other addicts in the household and you are trying to stay sober. Sometimes, even family members who are normal can be as strong a trigger as a sports bar or an invitation to snort a line at a party.

. . .

Once a man named Marco made an appointment to see
me because he was concerned about his wife. Elysa was a
film producer, hugely successful, and just turning fifty
years old. They had a strong marriage and two wonderful
children, but, he told me, she was an alcoholic. He was
concerned because she drove the kids in the car while she
was drunk, and it was becoming difficult for him to cope
with her drinking and do damage control. Elysa agreed to
come in for private sessions with me, although she continued to drink. After a couple of months, she hit bottom and
asked to be admitted to the Hills for inpatient treatment
for alcoholism. During the course of several weeks, Elysa
improved tremendously. She started to take control of her
family and her work, and, in sobriety, she started standing
up for herself. Now, Marco had always been the family's
knight in shining armor, the savior who excelled at taking
care of everything. As Elysa got healthier, her husband
found himself in a strange position, and he started to feel
threatened. Up until then, Marco had always been able to
blame Elysa's drinking for any problem in the family,
including his own issues. Marco started to sabotage Elysa
to "regain control," albeit killing her with kindness. He
bought groceries and restocked the refrigerator with alcohol, for example. Elysa relapsed, and Marco once again
came to the rescue. I started to see that the true "identified patient" here was Marco, not Elysa.

Elysa got sober again and continued to come in for
therapy. Marco, however, would not take part in our sessions. He was angry and in denial that he had any
problems. He continued to throw obstacles in the path of
Elysa's sobriety, which doubled or tripled her odds of
relapsing. Finally, I referred Marco to another therapist,

while I continued treating Elysa, and he eventually went in to get help for his own issues. Their marriage has survived, and it is stronger. He hadn't intended to hurt Elysa; he had only been acting out his own frustrations. They have both worked hard to rise above the challenges that were embedded in their unhealthy behavior.

· · ·

Here's What Can Help Prevent Relapse

The early stages of recovery are very dangerous terrain. Your brain chemicals are changing, and your behavioral routine is being retrained. You need constant balance, which is why community groups such as Alcoholics Anonymous are so valuable. Although avoiding trigger situations is vital to staying sober, there are proactive things you can do that will not only help you maintain sobriety, but will also build your sense of self. Your new drug of choice must be building self-esteem.

Flex Your Willpower Muscles

Research studies show that willpower can be limited, but only if we believe it is limited. Subjects in these studies proved that if they thought their willpower was finite, they ran out of it pretty quickly. Believing in infinite willpower actually builds an endless supply of it; it replenishes itself. That's not a spiritual adage, it's been proven in scientific studies. When you begin the motion of any activity, you build the energy to continue. When you resist one temptation, you can better resist the next one more easily. Willpower is all in your head, and you can strengthen it with time and practice. However, don't take it upon yourself to "test" your willpower by hanging out with people who are drinking and doing drugs. Give your willpower a little help.

Addiction expert Alan Marlatt at the University of Washington addressed an interesting phenomenon he called the "abstinence-violation effect." I call it the "fuck it effect." It's a form of black-and-white thinking, where you lose control if you slip just a little, so you proceed into an all-out binge.

"People with a strong abstinence-violation effect relapse much more quickly," Marlatt said. "A single slip solidifies their sense that they are a failure and cannot quit, creating a self-fulfilling prophecy."

Don't focus on whether you are strong enough to change. Focus on learning how to cope. It's like learning how to ride a bike. You don't just give up if you fall over once. And if the bicycle is broken, you cannot simply will it to work normally.

"Most people think that if they have urges or cravings, there's something wrong," said Marlatt. "In fact, they are a normal part of behavior. It's like a wave, it goes up and down. You don't try to get rid of it, but accept it and let it pass." Every time you let an urge pass without giving in to it, you strengthen your neural connections, and, with time, it gets easier to resist this urge. Marlatt created the acronym SOBER for his patients on how to fight the urge to slip:

Stop for a moment to think about what you're going.

Observe what you are feeling and experiencing.

Breathe.

Expand your awareness; remind yourself how you would feel afterward.

Respond mindfully and remember that you have a choice; you do not have to do something you know is wrong for you.

Be Proactive and Positive

Here's a good plan for dealing with temptation: Do something fearful first thing in the morning, and the adrenaline rush will keep you feeling good all day. Then get out of the house, go to work or go for a walk, and call a supportive friend. Live in the moment, but not if it's a negative moment. Move on, and quickly. It's not easy to maintain a positive attitude at all times, and no one expects you to. If you find yourself obsessing over a negative thought, call your sponsor or your therapist. Have that person on speed dial, because merely having him or her "on call" can build your ability to stay positive. When you are restless, you need company. Go find some.

Live in the Moment

When I refer to "living in the moment," what I really mean is don't be overconfident, because you might forget to be aware. You have to be ready to deal with stress as a sober person and maintain your healthy self-esteem. You should be proud of becoming sober and working through your issues. Yet having too much confidence can be dangerous—you might become complacent in your recovery. Feeling confidently sober is a good thing, but don't stop going to meetings or take your renewed self for granted. If you are overconfident, you may want to "prove" to someone that you can handle a drink or two.

Also, it's never a good idea to reminisce about the good old days of drinking and drugging. Sharing stories of high times may cause you to start obsessing about that time, and you need to move on. There's much to do in this world. You have better things to think about.

"They Would Stop If They Loved Me"

When we discover that a friend or a loved one is abusing drugs or alcohol, confusion is probably the most common reaction. Why is he doing this to himself? Doesn't she know how embarrassing this is for me? What did I do to make her become an addict? Surely, we think, if our friends or loved ones knew how painful it is for us to see them harm themselves this way, they would correct their behavior. Yet this is rarely the case. In the midst of addiction, your loved one will rarely change his or her reckless behavior for anyone or anything.

One of the most important things to remember when dealing with alcoholics or addicts is that they are not being addicts *at* you; they simply suffer from a disease, and their thoughts and behavior are governed by drugs or alcohol. Your brother did not miss your high school graduation to get high because he doesn't love you. Your mother didn't total the car while driving drunk because she wanted to scare you. Your friend didn't sleep through your recital because you are a bad musician—this behavior is the direct result of addiction, which requires constant and vigilant maintenance, often at the expense of others.

Sobriety also requires constant and vigilant maintenance. If the addict or the alcoholic chases his sobriety the way he chases his drugs, he'll be in great shape. He will, on a moment-to-moment basis, strive to improve his life, his perception, his gratitude, and his usefulness to others. Unfortunately, no one but the addict can determine when he is ready to change his life for the better; alcoholism is a self-diagnosed disease. When your friend or loved one begins living in recovery, however, he will be healthier, happier, and more open to receiving your love and support.

Stay in Therapy

Now that you are sober, you have a world of emotional issues to confront without using the numbing agents of drugs and alcohol. It might also be revealed that you have manic depression or some other psychological condition that caused your addictions in the first place. You may find that other family members are causing problems for you, and all of you need to learn how to resolve conflicts in healthy ways. Continue weekly appointments with your therapist for at least a year or two after getting sober, as well as group meetings. This will complete your healing and provide the coping tools that are your insurance. It is an investment that will pay off for the rest of your life.

Have Patience

Patients and their family members all need a lot of patience as they wait for the healing to set in. Emotions are volatile, insomnia is rampant, and patients start to feel as if they will be miserable for the rest of their lives. Their loved ones may misinterpret agitation or emotional outbursts as signs that the patients are still being irresponsible.

Sometimes I think that the *fear* of relapse is more paralyzing than relapse itself. People in the addict's life are on constant vigil, thinking, "Is he late because he's out drinking?" No one needs to assume that relapse will happen, and there is no point in constantly worrying about it.

If you, the patient, get bored, join a health club, start playing softball with sober friends, or plan a trip to a foreign country. Don't start to feel sorry for yourself. Life may not be fair if you can't drink as other people can, but there is a huge world of things to do, other than drink or use drugs.

Sleep

Sleep is the most healthy function of the human body. Sure, we need to exercise and eat healthy foods, but nothing we can do has the health-restorative benefits of simple sleep. Someone who is drunk or high needs only to get some sleep in order to be restored to sobriety. No food or pill has this effect. Teenagers require more sleep than the rest of us, but our overall sleep patterns keep us healthy for a lifetime. As addicts, of course, many of us have lost the ability to get enough rest. Our abuse of drugs and alcohol has totally untrained our bodies in the art of falling asleep. We have tampered with our brain chemistry.

Rapid eye movement (REM) sleep is a period of deep healing for all of us, but particularly for an alcoholic or an addict. During deep sleep and REM sleep, the brain regulates all of its chemicals and resets the neurotransmitter systems. Without enough sleep, we are unable to focus, we have poor memory, and our minds do not function properly. Those in recovery should get at least eight hours of sleep per night. If you are in your teens or twenties, I even recommend ten hours a night.

On the road to getting clean and sober, sleep often becomes an issue. Insomnia can last for several months. Taking prescription trazodone or melatonin can help you reestablish healthy sleep patterns.

It also helps to participate in a 12-step program. Consistent therapy and group counseling during the early months of recovery will help you reestablish healthy sleep cycles and help heal the changes to your brain chemistry. Some of the patients who have insomnia are not the addicts themselves, but their family members. There are many avenues that family members can pursue to find healing for themselves, as well as for their loved ones who are addicts.

One of the most rejuvenating and energizing things we can do is get some sleep. None of us gets enough rest. The early stages of sobriety may cause insomnia in some of us, but continued therapy can address this issue and help you learn how to maximize your sleeping hours. I don't recommend that you sleep during the day, however, and isolate yourself from the rest of the waking world. In addition, studies have found that the body produces large amounts of melatonin only when you sleep during the dark hours of the night, with all of the lights turned off in your room. Adequate bodily levels of melatonin have been found to protect against cancer and various other diseases. So, you should get enough sleep at night, at least eight hours, maybe even ten—whatever makes you feel best. I don't understand why some people think it's morally questionable to sleep long hours at night. If you can get it, take it, and don't let anyone make you feel guilty about it. Sleeping is the most restorative thing you can do for your body. People who need the most sleep are teenagers and young adults. Don't give the kids grief about sleeping a lot.

Insomnia is a stressful condition, but you can take steps to lessen your insomnia. Try some of these helpful ideas in order to get more sleep.

Glorious Sleep

- Try to go to bed and wake up at the same times every day. A regular routine is one of the best ways to maintain good sleep habits.
- Reading or watching TV can help you become drowsy. When you nod off, turn out the lights and go to sleep.
- Don't watch or read anything stressful or exciting late at night.
- Check your medications. Ask your doctor if one of your meds might be responsible for interrupting your sleep.
- Sometimes, changing where you sleep can help you rest better. Try the sofa or a guest bed, or simply rearrange the furniture in your room. I don't recommend sleeping in a chair.
- Try taking a melatonin tablet before bedtime or a calcium tablet.
- Don't look at the clock in the middle of the night. Hide the clock. You can still set the alarm, but put the time out of sight.

- Go for a walk or work out, preferably just before or after eating dinner. This will wear your body out, and it will put you into a deeper sleep.
- Avoid caffeine and cigarettes—and, needless to say, alcohol and drugs.
- Close your bedroom door.
- Some people swear by "white noise," such as a fan.
- Change your schedule: try to stay awake an hour longer, and let yourself sleep an hour later in the morning. The sun's schedule for rising and setting affects each of us differently, so altering your own habits might induce more sleep.
- If you have insomnia at night, don't take naps during the day.
- Turn your thermostat down at night.
- Do not work or brainstorm before bedtime—the goal is to relax your mind and not think of anything agitating or stressful.
- Take a hot bath or a hot shower just before bedtime.
- Drink hot chamomile tea or the proverbial warm milk. Or both!
- Concentrate on your breathing. Listen to your body as you inhale and exhale. When a thought enters your mind, banish it. Listen to your breath.
- Tell the "beast" chatter in your brain to be quiet. Sometimes a conscious announcement to "shut up" will help make it happen.
- Consult your doctor, if all else fails. It is possible that a prescription for Lunesta or trazodone might help you, if you really need it.

Oh, Yeah—Avoid Being around Alcohol and Drugs

You can still be crazy, funny, daring, and cool. Your life can still be full—actually, more full—of great times and memorable people and places. That's good crazy. Recovering addicts are probably the most fun, smart, and entertaining people I know. Half of the productions in Hollywood are now made by creative, edgy people who are sober. I know this because they're all at my AA meetings. Go to your meetings. You don't have to think of them as "repairing a negative aspect in your life." Think of meetings as adding enormous benefits to your life. They provide you with commiseration and humor, networking for jobs and friendships, support and advice for everyday life, and healthy, honest interactions with good people in your own community.

You don't need to go to bars and nightclubs, though, or hang out with the party crowd in their dens of iniquity. I am a huge sports fan, and the idea of a sports bar crowd watching a New York Giants game has great appeal for me. But I don't need to go to a bar to have a great time watching the Giants. I watch the game with friends at home or go to the stadium with my son, and I make it an event where we all have a good time. As a sober man, I have way more appreciation for the players and the game than I ever did when I was high all of the time. Football is a passion I discovered when I got sober. Think of all of the new things you can do, now that you've stopped wasting time doing all of that other crap.

Wanting something is okay. Don't feel bad if you have that gut reaction sometimes. Wanting is okay, but needing is not. I still have trigger moments. With time and practice, I hardly even notice them anymore.

Realize That Your Symptoms Are Normal

Your emotions are sensitive in early recovery, because they are no longer covered up by your substance abuse. This can be overwhelming for some people who are not used to dealing with their feelings; they might get depressed or have thoughts of resentment. It is normal to feel this way. Your feelings will gradually start to calm down. Almost all addicts experience new emotions and feelings that they hadn't been dealing with while in active addiction. You might actually start to embrace these emotions when you can respond in a healthy way.

Physical symptoms of early recovery will also start to disappear, such as insomnia, decreased appetite, restlessness, chills, headaches, muscular and joint pain, mood swings, a decrease in energy, and an inability to focus. Your body will start to feel better. Exercise releases natural endorphins in the body and can improve your mood, as well as your overall well-being.

PART THREE

For Family and Friends

11

Taking Steps to Intervene

Maurice and Anne K. are college professors in their forties who live with their two teenagers, Alec and Sam, in a lovely home. In the last four years, the K's have had two cars destroyed, paid $20,000 to a bail bondsman, and paid another $60,000 to a local attorney. They have overdue hospital bills for roughly $15,000 and spent their children's college funds to pay for rehab for the rambunctious Sam, their high school senior. Everyone loves Sam, but he clearly has a problem with drinking. Maurice and Anne are hoping Sam will grow out of it soon. Alec, meanwhile, is more serious, although he gets only Cs in his tenth-grade classes. Alec spends most of his time in his room, listening to music and surfing the Internet, away from the drama downstairs. Anne has lost a lot of time at work, and Maurice almost never comes home from his office anymore.

Karen O. is a thirty-five-year-old single mother with a twelve-year-old daughter, Jasmine, and a full-time job. Her sister, thirty-three-year-old Krystal, moved in last year, so Karen's daughter moved over to share Karen's room. Krystal can't keep a job but has a lot of friends who drive her to clubs, and she parties every night. She sleeps all day and watches television with Jasmine after school. Karen loves her sister but has spent her entire life making excuses for Krystal in the hopes that, one day, Krystal will "find herself" and make a happy life. Meanwhile, Krystal smokes a lot of pot in her bedroom, and Karen now wonders if this is a good example for Jasmine. Karen doesn't want to think about the two occasions when she noticed cash missing from her purse.

Jeri is a wealthy fifty-year-old divorcee. She is lonely and doesn't mind that her twenty-one-year-old son, Jacob, still lives at home. Her ex-husband, a doctor, left her for a younger woman three years earlier. There's plenty of room in the large house, and her son leads a life indepen-dent from hers. Jeri has many friends and stays busy organizing charity events. Once in a while, she takes a Vicodin to comfort herself in the evening. She has a long-time prescription. Unbeknownst to her, but evident to most other people who know them, Jacob has a heroin habit, on which he is spending $600 a day.

Mark J. is a professional athlete who was arrested for his third DUI and thrown in jail. His wife is long gone, because he hasn't stopped partying since 1999. Mark's grown daughter hired a costly attorney who made a deal with prosecutors: Mark can go to rehab instead of prison. He's relieved, because rehab is better than prison, but he's still in denial that he has a problem with drinking.

●   ●   ●

In the beginning, it is normal for family members to ignore or rationalize the behavior of the addict; they want to protect the one they love. There is little distinction between the substances being abused: these family dynamics play out whether it is an alcoholic, an addict using prescription painkillers, pot-smoking teens, or homeless street junkies who do not even live in the house anymore. I could list additional symptoms to look for: behavioral problems, learning disabilities, job complaints, poor impulse control, mood swings, lying, stealing, or problems with the law. If you are reading this book, though, you have already identified that the problem exists. Your family is being affected by addiction.

Adding to the challenge of finding help, addiction is vilified by many in a way that other chronic illnesses are not, which often makes it hard for the family to reach out. On top of that, many professionals and medical doctors are not well informed about the best ways to seek effective treatment for addiction. There is no national board certification, association, or professional over-sight in this field. Hard to believe, but it's true. Certain states have "certification" requirements, which are comparable to obtaining a general business license, such as for a pawn shop or a beauty salon. Medical schools cover certain physiological and even psychological aspects of addiction, in terms of patient care, but do not begin to address the issue of family assistance and lifetime therapies. Little wonder it is so hard for a family to know where to turn.

Treating addiction and alcoholism is difficult enough, even for a professional like me with tons of experience. You and your family cannot do it on your own. Whether it's your son, daughter, spouse, parent, or close friend, there is no enforcement agency or social group that will fix this problem for you. The only ones who will make the calls and confront the patient will be members of the family.

Warning Signs for Teen Drug Abuse

Physical: Fatigue, unusual sleep patterns, small or "pinned" pupils, large pupils, constant sickness, consistent cough, and/or red or glazed eyes.

Emotional: Personality change, mood swings, irritability, unresponsive behavior, low self-esteem, poor judgment, depression, and a general lack of interest.

School: Decreased interest, negative attitude, drop in academic performance, absences, truancy, and discipline problems.

Social issues: Changing friends, problems with the law, less conventional styles of dress and music.

Family: Isolating themselves from the family, starting arguments with family members, breaking rules.

I emphasize the importance of finding someone who is a psychotherapist and, preferably, who is a recovered addict him- or herself. Some addicts need treatment from a medical doctor to wean themselves off the substances, in which case, your therapist will help you find one. The Resources at the back of this book provides details on how to find the appropriate psychotherapist in your area. You will have better luck confronting your loved one if you are prepared with information and have professional support already lined up. The following sections explain how you can be prepared.

First, Understand the Situation

As you may know by now, the primary thing to remember is that addicts and alcoholics can't just quit whenever they want to. They do not lack willpower or morals but are suffering from a serious disease. They cannot change how their brains are misfiring. The addict may want to change, may vow to change, and may even stop using for a while. Yet a buried psychological issue inside him or her, as well as an established chemical imbalance, always leads back to self-destruction. Your loved one is very ashamed of his or her behavior. You need to understand that this disease is not the addict's fault, and it's also not your fault.

Many times, it is parents who come to me in desperation. This is usually not their first attempt to intervene with their child; they've "tried everything." Yet they haven't given up. In my own case, I didn't go to rehab until my family told me they wouldn't support me anymore. They wouldn't give me money, they wouldn't talk to me on the phone, and they wouldn't give me a place to live. They were loving; they didn't pile on the shame and the guilt. They just pulled the plug. You know what? It worked. Well-meaning parents who give their kids money or free living accommodations are making a mistake, in my opinion. I believe that whether or not there are addiction problems, parents think they're being supportive when they support an adult child—though they are frequently alleviating some guilt of their own— but it is actually a great hindrance to teaching the child responsibility.

Rest assured, no matter what your relationship is like with the addict, you are doing the right thing by getting involved and taking action. It is better to face the problem than continue to avoid it. Arm yourself with plenty of patience, because it will take a few weeks to find and meet with a therapist and to feel as if you have made any progress. Be hopeful, because you have every reason to believe that your family will be healed, and your faith in the outcome plays a role in making it happen. Also, remember to be grateful, because your loved one is still alive. There are many other families who wish they had taken action before it was too late.

Be Prepared: Consult a Professional

The Resources at the back of this book shows you where to find experts in your area. It is also good to ask friends for recommendations, as well as medical providers or school counselors. Whether it's your spouse, child, or parent, here are a few considerations to help you narrow down your options:

1. Look for someone who has experience with treating addiction. Many therapists and medical doctors believe they can treat addicts and may provide real help, but this is a hugely challenging specialty. Someone who has treated alcoholics and addicts understands this and tends to stay with the patient for the long haul.

2. Look for a therapist who is a recovering addict or alcoholic him- or herself. This means that the therapist not only understands the challenges of recovery, but can better gain the respect of the patient. This therapist can say, "I have been there," which carries enormous impact for an addict. No fancy medical degree or hospital association carries this much weight, in the eyes of a patient, and for good reason.

3. A good counselor will treat the whole family. I believe an alcoholic or an addict should initially see a counselor every day or enter a live-in rehab facility. Once or twice a week, the whole family should join in. This enhances the treatment of the patient, who learns how to reestablish

healthy family dynamics. Of course, this also benefits the other family members, who are tired and confused, and who need to learn new behavior in the household in order to assist the recovering family member.

4. Find someone who will treat the addict even if the addict is still using drugs and alcohol. Many therapists "cut off" a patient who slips and insist on complete sobriety before they will allow further consultation. I think this is an enormous miscalculation on the part of the therapist. We know the patient is going to struggle in the early weeks and months—the best therapist understands that relapse is part of the process (and, hopefully, the patient will survive the relapse). When I take on a new client, I often "fasten my seat belt" for a wild ride until the patient finally hits the wall. That wall might be prison or the hospital or a psychic shift such as I had when my father died. An experienced counselor will recognize the lies and the manipulation of a patient who is still using but will stay involved for the many months it may take for the addict to reach sobriety.

5. Look for a therapist who endorses a 12-step program as an adjunct to regular therapy. If the counselor is a recovering addict him- or herself, this individual is well aware of the importance of community support, not only for the patient but for the other family members as well. It doesn't have to be Alcoholics Anonymous, but any sort of 12-step group will enhance the addict's treatment and recovery. I cannot tell you how many cases I have seen end in failure because no one thought that the 12-step support system was important. I am here to assure you that it is vital to your loved one's success, and any effective counselor will agree.

Here are things that are not important when choosing a therapist: where the therapist went to school or what kind of degree he or she earned. If the professional charges excessive fees, then seek out a therapist who costs less or one who will accept extended payments. If you do not like the first therapist you visit, then seek out another one. If you "like" the therapist, but he or she doesn't seem to provide tangible assistance, then seek out another one. If you don't like the second or third one you meet, then continue to "interview" new therapists.

Having someone to support your actions will help give you confidence in talking to your loved one. If you have a friend you can trust, you may be surprised to learn that he or she has information about where to find help. Sometimes you have a family doctor who can make referrals for you, but other times you don't. Consult school guidance counselors, who often have a treasure trove of resources, as well as other parents who can provide support. Look at the websites listed in the back of this book, which provide resource assistance no matter where you live. Alternatively, check your local listings for "Drug Abuse" and "Mental Health." Many people may consult their clergy, hospitals, or local police.

At your first appointment, it is important to tell the therapist absolutely everything—the family history and all about the abuser's behavior, the arrests, the school records, previous attempts to treat the addict, and the emotional state of the rest of the family. One mother felt that it was not her place to tell the counselor all about her son's drug use and bad behavior. Mom felt as if it was some sort of invasion of privacy because he was twenty-one and he had "rights." She felt that her addicted son was responsible enough to disclose all of his substance abuse to the counselor, even though he had been known to lie and steal from his family for years. Evidently, some families will even use amendments to the U.S. Constitution as an excuse to remain in denial. You can be certain that addicts will hide their problems from everyone who asks, especially a counselor, because they have been doing so for a long time, and they know no other behavior. The patients are very ashamed of their behavior, and the parents also feel ashamed and guilty. The right psychotherapist will understand that the addict's lies and manipulation may continue for a while.

Talk about It; Listen Even More

Bringing up the subject of addiction with the addict requires a great deal of diplomacy and courage. No one wants to be the one who brings it up. You don't want to hurt the addict or the alcoholic or make that person angry and defensive. Addicts and their families sometimes resist taking action because they think it is impossible for a person to change. You—and he or she—must believe that there is a chance of success.

Turn off the television and the Internet. Remember that your loved one is accustomed to hearing advice from you, so he or she needs to understand that this conversation is serious. This is not the time to tell your own stories. This conversation must allow the addicts to speak, too. They are not accustomed to feeling "understood"; they might get angry with you.

Ask questions they can answer, such as:

"Can you tell me more about what you did last night?"

"I'm concerned about the things you and your friends do— what can we do about that?"

"I am concerned with how much drinking and drug use is going on at your school. How are you coping with that?"

"I trust you to do the right thing, but I'm the parent, and it's my job to be concerned."

Don't ask, "Why did you go out drinking?" because the addicts probably don't know the answer. You must accept that not only can you *not* control their behavior, but sometimes even *they* can't control their behavior. In this conversation, you are the responsible one, but the conversation is not about you.

Remain calm, and try not to sound disapproving or judgmental. Hang in there, and keep your own words to a minimum. Wait through the silences. Many people don't want to talk "on command." Your loved one may respond with anger, which is masking great fear. Don't respond with more impatience and anger. Just keep listening. Don't deflect when the addict accuses you—listen with respect, even if you are uncomfortable. If you speak too much, this sends mixed messages, and you want to have a discussion, not a confrontation. Nothing should be hidden, even if it is about alcohol, drugs, stealing, or sex. Whenever possible, praise your loved one for being communicative and for achieving positive milestones, for speaking honestly.

It is helpful to come prepared with examples of success. I have learned that stories from other people often get through to a patient, as long as these stories are not about you yourself. Don't say, "When I was your age." You could bring up stories about other friends or even from the newspaper. "I read about a young man who lost his best friend to a drug overdose and then started a charity to educate school kids on the dangers of drugs."

Trust your instincts and knowledge—you know more than you think. You may not be an expert in addiction treatment, but you are a caring family member who can do a lot of good—the most good. No matter how long it's been going on or how much devastation has occurred, it is never too late.

It will probably take several conversations before the addict or the alcoholic will get comfortable with the topic or even admit that he or she might need help. Don't be discouraged if it takes a while: a few weeks, months even. That is part of the process.

There are two kinds of people who really need to go to rehab:

1. Addicts or alcoholics who know nothing about the recovery process, aka the "virgins." Their whole lives are in need of overhaul, and they need a shift in their thinking twenty-four hours a day, seven days a week.

2. Those who can't stop using on their own. Therapy and outpatient therapy are simply not enough for many addicts. They may have already tried several times, and they keep relapsing. They need to go back again.

Intervene

Sometimes, families don't want to wait until there's a car accident or an arrest to convince the addict to get professional help and psychotherapy. In many cases, families fear someone will die before their loved one gets help, that this person will never "hit bottom" because it's been bad for so long. To avert a crisis, it is perfectly acceptable to retain a rehab counselor who will instruct the family members on how to confront the addict in an intervention. It takes a couple weeks of planning, and the counselor will assist friends and family members in preparing a list of incidents that will convince the patient that he or she needs help. The therapist will coach the attendees about not being judgmental or accusing.

If you are a concerned family member who wants to arrange an intervention, in order to be successful, I strongly advise that you do not even begin without a good therapist on your team. It is difficult enough as it is; without a properly trained professional, your odds of success are diminished. Before the intervention, your family and loved ones should meet and discuss what will happen during the intervention. First, set a time and a place for the intervention to occur. You must create a way to bring the addict to the location without arousing suspicion. Next, choose a leader.

Optimally, a therapist or an interventionist will guide the entire process. Don't take this on yourselves. And keep trying. It took my family members several interventions with me. They didn't give up, and ultimately their intervention saved my life. Don't give up. Continue the pressure on your loved one. Even the addict's awareness of your concern will start to have an influence.

Ask the people who will attend the intervention to each prepare a statement or a letter to the addict, perhaps mentioning how they have seen the person change as a result of his or her addiction, how the person's addiction has affected them, what they are asking the addict to do, and what the consequences will be if the addict does not go into treatment.

When the addict arrives at the designated time and place, he or she typically is caught off guard. Arranging the intervention to be a surprise prevents the addict from having time to come up with excuses to avoid it. Ask your loved one to sit down and simply listen to what all of you have to say. If the addict reacts with anger or intensity, remain calm. After the addict has agreed to listen to what family members have to say, people in the group should takes turns reading their statements. Addicts will ideally become aware of how much their addiction has affected their own lives, as well as the lives of people around them. Then, give the addict an ultimatum: either go into treatment, or be prepared to deal with new boundaries that you have set in place.

This is not an easy thing to do, for anyone involved. You care about this person, but if you care enough, you will make the extraordinary effort to help your loved one. If the addict then chooses to go to treatment, support him through the process. Addiction is a family disease and affects everyone. If the individual is not willing to go to treatment, family members should stand firm with the ultimatums they have laid out.

Interventions have proved to be a relatively successful way to get someone into treatment. Although they are often met with resentment or anger at first, this usually fades quickly. As the addicts get sober and gain a clearer picture of what had been happening in their lives, they become grateful to the participants in the intervention for their care and love.

Intervention Step by Step

1. Meet with friends and family members, but do not include the addict or the alcoholic. Between three and six people is a good number. Agree that you will maintain confidentiality, and please do not include children. Discuss the facts about the patient, and note the harmful behavior all of you observe. Plan what each of you will say and in what order. Try not to be repetitive. Discuss how you believe the patient will react, and anticipate how you will address denials, tears, anger, and so forth.

2. Meet with a professional counselor or therapist before the intervention, with your whole group but not with the patient. Rehearse what each of you will say, and discuss possible reactions with the therapist. The therapist may ask that you write down a list of behaviors that will no longer be tolerated and what the consequences will be if each behavior continues. You might also make a list of losses that resulted from the addict's behavior, such as a job, a relationship, or money. Choose a spokesperson for the intervention.

3. Discuss treatment options with the therapist. Ascertain that the situation merits intervention, that the patient is causing harm but is otherwise not suffering from a mental condition. Choose a facility in advance, and contact that facility to discuss your plan.

4. Choose a private location, and decide who will sit where. Make sure there will be no interruptions,

including cell phones. All should be in attendance before the patient arrives. Arrange a time when you believe the patient will be sober.

5. When the patient arrives, speak calmly and do not accuse anyone in the room. "We are all here because we love you and we are concerned about you." You don't need to use the words *addict* or *alcoholic*. Begin each sentence with the word I or we, and not the word you. Such as, "I am upset about how you are drinking and stressing out the family," or "We are here to save you from yourself."

6. Ask the patient to confirm that there is a problem. If he or she denies a problem, go around the room and ask each group member for evidence of the problem. Remember to avoid accusations or anger. Listen to what the addict says, but don't agree with him or her. Tell the addict you love him or her, and that you don't want the addict to destroy his or her life.

7. Offer immediate treatment, and explain the details about the therapeutic facility you have arranged. It is not acceptable for the patient to say that he or she will seek treatment "later." This meeting is an ultimatum, and you have prepared in advance for what you will say to every objection. It will be difficult, but the counselor will help the patient deal with anger or denial. You don't want the patient to feel as if everyone has ganged up on him or her, but be strong. Don't cave in.

8. Close the meeting on a positive note: "We just care so much about you, or we wouldn't do this at all." In most cases, the patient will agree to go to rehab. If not, then that doesn't mean you failed. Your efforts may start a chain of events that ultimately leads to change for the patient. In addition, you have made it known that you will no longer enable his or her behavior.

An intervention is a success even if the client refuses to go to rehab, because at least the family has united to set a boundary. This means life will not be the same for the addict, and a process has started that will one day result in the addict getting treatment.

Outpatient Rehab

Most therapists will propose that your loved one enter a rehab program. In some cases, my patients enter rehabilitation because they broke the law. They are arrested for DUI, for possession, or from a hospital bed after a car accident. Sound familiar? Instead of going to prison, many offenders are permitted to "serve time" by getting psychiatric treatment for their substance abuse. I talk to scores of probation officers and judges on a weekly basis. Many communities and hospitals have "outpatient rehab" facilities that require daily attendance but allow the patient to live at home. These programs may vary between two weeks and six months and are often covered by your insurance policy. I might recommend outpatient rehab five days a week if the addict has been sober for a few months already.

If you or your loved one is truly addicted, however, I recommend inpatient rehab. There are just too many ways for an addict to obtain illicit substances if he or she is living at home.

Inpatient Rehab

In many cases, your family member cannot adhere to a program or outpatient therapy. It is very helpful for that person to enter a residential facility where there are twenty-four-hour attendants to care for the patient. Inpatient rehab centers help teach the patient a whole new way of life, one without drugs and alcohol and with more self-esteem and a sense of responsibility. The old-fashioned "boot camp" facilities have been replaced by centers such as the Hills, where patients work in the garden, do yoga, and clean the kitchen in between therapy sessions and classes. Many rehab centers use what is now known as the "Minnesota Model," so named because it was the state where Alcoholics Anonymous first flourished and where the Hazelden clinic found success. Their programs include sobriety, of course, as well as reeducation and therapy, daily visits to local AA meetings, school (if necessary), recreational therapy, and family counseling. Most of them do not use medications at all, unless there is a need for withdrawal meds or there is a dual diagnosis of depression or bipolar disease.

Many patients who are addicted to prescription medications, tranquilizers, or narcotics need medical supervision, which inpatient facilities provide. These patients have damaged brain receptors and require special therapy to work on relearning cognitive behavior, in addition to withdrawing from drugs. Patients going through withdrawal have physical reactions, such as headaches, nausea, insomnia, and stomach cramps, as well as mental reactions, such as hallucinations, paranoia, anxiety, and even seizures. There are modern medical treatments that reduce the discomfort of withdrawal, but it must be safely achieved before therapy can even begin.

Parents can't be therapists. If your child is seventeen years of age or younger, you can send the child to a rehabilitation center without his or her approval. If children are eighteen or older, they must be willing to enter treatment and cannot be forced to enter any type of program. Even if your child is seventeen or younger, it is ideal if he or she is willing to get help. Yet the truth is, most patients who are in rehab don't want to be there. We work on their denial every day.

Inpatient facilities can be found in the Resources at the back of this book and also through referrals made by your friends and doctors. A counselor or an admissions director at the center will recommend the length of stay, but it is not unusual to be a minimum of two months and as long as eighteen months. The minimum of two months ensures a physical withdrawal, at least, but it should be followed up by several more months in a sober living facility and psychotherapy. In other words, unless it is for at least a year, inpatient rehab is not "enough," in most cases. These facilities provide group therapy on a daily basis, private therapy, family counseling, strict routines for activities and outings, sober companions for off-site visits, participation in Alcoholics Anonymous or Narcotics Anonymous, doctors' examinations, and round-the-clock support. It is expensive, but it is the best investment you can make for your loved one who is addicted.

Families should not have to go broke while paying for treatment. Look for a rehab center that gives a refund if the client leaves early. No family should be punished financially if the patient leaves early! The family has been punished enough. Some treatment centers care a little too much about your money. I know of one center that charged a family $50,000 for six months of outpatient treatment. The client left after one week and never returned. The treatment center did not refund the deposit, which, I believe, simply caused further stress to the whole family. Read the fine print of any contract at a treatment facility.

Find a program that you can afford, preferably one that is based on the 12 steps. If it does not use the 12 steps, it will be a waste of money. Trust me, I have learned this from experience. Although modern facilities may have amenities such as swimming pools and gourmet food, they are institutions. The patients are not coming for a vacation. They are in rehab to do some very difficult work.

Remember, a treatment center does not "fix" your loved one. We stabilize addicts and set them on the right track for the rest of their lives. The program at our facility, the Hills, focuses on the big picture, above and beyond substance abuse. Who are we? What are we doing? What values are we teaching? Once patients are newly sober, they must learn to redefine their purpose in life, their sense of self, and their personal goals. A good therapist will provide this sort of guidance on an outpatient basis as well. Not only that, but most inpatient facilities will help establish a sober living arrangement for patients who move onward in sobriety. This sets them up with roommates who are also in recovery, and residents can share rides to group meetings and provide supportive and sober companionship to events and activities in the outside world. Many college campuses now have dormitories that are for students in recovery, in addition to dorms that are merely designated as free of alcohol and drugs.

Wilderness Therapy

Wilderness programs are an adventure-based therapy with outdoor expeditions for the purpose of therapeutic treatment. The goal of these programs is to teach self-respect and self-reliance to teens who have substance abuse and behavioral problems. There are different types of wilderness programs that range from more intensive survival-based therapy to the Outward Bound approach. The goal of these programs is to change the outlook of the client. Leaving behind material items such as cell phones, computers, and television, teens are reduced to the bare minimum and learn character building. Separating these individuals from negative peers also allows them to shed their "image," which is a big part of this therapeutic treatment. Activities include learning survival skills, hiking, cooking, building structures, and learning how to be self-reliant in a strange situation. These programs promote recovery with the underlying roots of the 12-step fellowship, while implementing the therapeutic values of the great outdoors.

I have a former patient, Kevin, who was seventeen and simply couldn't kick heroin. His family sent him to a rigorous outdoor program in Colorado. The experience changed his life, not only because he got clean and learned how to empower himself, but also because he made great friends, learned to ski, and enrolled in college in Colorado. He has been sober now for eleven years.

There are many different wilderness programs, which differ in approach and style of therapy. All of these programs teach valuable tools and can help change the perspective of teenagers or young adults and refocus them on the things in life that are important.

Be Supportive, Cautiously

If your loved one has completed rehab and needs a place to live while he or she continues recovery, then by all means be supportive. If that person is attending counseling and AA meetings and working on a productive life, your emotional and even financial support shows that you are proud of his or her progress and are building trust between the two of you. Unless it is your spouse, the patient should not live with you after rehab. It is important for that loved one to live in a sober environment and be self-supporting as much as possible, to learn responsibility and gain self-esteem.

Don't support any child or sibling who is still using, no matter what his or her age. You are supporting the child's habit. Give the child the option to stop using and get treatment; otherwise, he or she must be cut off from your support.

If your loved one is not working on recovery, the family should not provide any support except love. Don't give addicts a place to live, money, or even conversation, unless they are actively participating in their recovery and working on a productive life. You don't have to nag. Just pull the plug, with love, not shame or anger. Allow your loved one to hit another bottom, if necessary. If your child or loved one is not attending regular AA meetings, do not give him or her money or a place to live. We have learned that such support is counterproductive. The person who is financially supported without rehabilitation will go back to drinking and drugging, without question.

You can do plenty of other things to be supportive while you and the patient begin treatment. Because you are getting treatment for yourself as well, you can consult the therapist on proper ways to respond to your loved one.

Whether it is your spouse, your sibling, or your child, don't argue with the addict or accuse him or her of lying, and don't "lay down the law." This immediately puts your loved one on the defensive. You, like the therapist, need to form an alliance with your loved one, to battle the disease. Family conversations are learned—and maybe your own parents weren't that great at communicating with you when you were young. It takes time to build trust between the two of you.

People who are going to drop out of rehab typically do so within ninety days. That three-month period is when it is most vital for you to be supportive of your loved one and encourage his or her progress. Those who stay in a program for the full term are more likely to recover. If your family member discontinues rehab, don't be discouraged. The patient will be welcomed back without judgment when he or she is ready to try again.

What's with All the Red Bull?

We have seen celebrities from Britney Spears and Paris Hilton to Demi Moore chugging from a little blue-and-silver can of Red Bull, an Austrian beverage that contains mostly caffeine and sugar. Athletes also use it the way they drink Gatorade, for an energy boost. I suspect that the partying Hollywood types drink it so they can keep partying longer. It is not, in itself, addictive. One can of Red Bull contains about the same amount of caffeine as a cup of coffee and about seven teaspoons of sugar. Drinks such as Jolt and Monster contain even higher amounts of caffeine and sugar. Red Bull also contains taurine, an amino acid that is important for neurological development, and it seriously raises your blood pressure, so much so that it has been banned, on and off, in countries such as France and Norway.

We don't allow Red Bull at the Hills—it is simply an intense stimulant that releases dopamine, and it is very appealing to those recovering from cocaine or methamphetamine addiction. We don't need our patients to replace one toxic stimulant with another. Coffee in moderation is okay; sugar is okay. But water is better.

Don't be afraid to be the "bad parent," even if the addict is your sister or your father. Fear of a negative reaction will sometimes stop a parent from taking a tough stand. You are in charge! When there's an addict in the house, your family is not a democracy. Learning how to say no may not be fun, but it is required if drinking and drugging have already entered the family dynamic.

House rules allow family members to use the rules as a reason to say no to drinking and drugging. You have to learn how to say a definitive no. Make clear rules for your household. no drinking alcohol unless you are twenty-one, no riding in a car with anyone who has been drinking, older siblings may not engage younger ones in drinking or using drugs, and your children under twenty-one must promise not to attend any party where alcohol or drugs are present or a parent is absent. Set a curfew. Expect decent grades at school.

If any of the rules are broken, even once, there must be ramifications. Take away the cell phone for an evening, turn off the television and the computer, take away the car. It might be helpful to change schools if your child cannot avoid peers who drink and use drugs. Don't try to be your teenager's friend or cave in to his or her threats. As the parent, you are allowed to be tough. Tell kids why their behavior is wrong, and that you're disappointed when they break the rules. You still love them, and you will give them another chance to succeed. Hug your kids, and praise them for all of the good things they do. Be proud that they are getting help.

Revive the family meal, and encourage everyone to contribute. You don't have to do what my Dad did and ask, "What did you do today to be productive?" That invites a suggestion of failure. Ask instead, "What are we grateful for today?" and "What are our goals for tomorrow?"

Studies show that parents' expectations play a huge role in what their teens do. It is not a good thing to overlook or write off teenage drinking or drug use as normal experimentation. Many parents believe this is inevitable. Not so. It is not just a phase that "all kids go through"—you are simply making excuses that enable their behavior. A passive attitude proves to be a self-fulfilling prophecy. Studies show that parents who expect their teens to try alcohol or drugs have children who are ten times more likely to do so, as opposed to those who say their kids will never do it before the age of twenty-one.

To that end, you may want to consider a "family contract," which lays out the rules of what you expect from the young adult who lives in your home. Maybe you don't really need to write it down, but you can have discussions about setting curfews, meal times, and homework hours; using the car; doing chores; attending counseling appointments; engaging in respectful behavior toward everyone in the house; and of course, not using drugs or alcohol.

If your loved one becomes violent or threatening, no matter where he or she lives, you should call someone for help immediately: the police or a family friend. We know that young people can become obsessed about suicide, and more than half of our teens who kill themselves also had issues with drugs or alcohol. This does not mean that drugs made them want to commit suicide, only that drugs may well have exacerbated an already existing condition. If you notice startling changes, such as severe mood swings or a sudden interest in death, seek immediate help from a professional. Please bear in mind that very few young people who are abusing drugs and alcohol are suicidal; these symptoms also exist in teens who are clean and sober. It's safest to leave the assessment to a professional. That is the best thing you can do, as a parent.

Being a Role Model

Be a role model—what you do is more important than what you say. Never is this adage more true than when it comes to drinking. If you drink, chances are, your child will drink. Teens who believe that their parents are "okay with" their drinking are nearly three times more likely to get drunk in a typical month than are those who believe their parents would not approve. More often than with mothers, fathers tacitly communicate that it is okay for a teen to drink. That unspoken approval is all teens need to get started.

Be aware of how you talk to your spouse and what your own drinking routines are in the home. The kids are learning most of their behavior from you. If your son or daughter starts to mention someone in school who is having problems with drugs or drinking, pay attention. They may be subconsciously telling you something that is true about themselves. Keep tabs on your alcohol and also on your prescription drugs. Home is the first place where young people obtain these substances.

People sometimes forget to acknowledge that getting drunk or high can feel pretty good, plain and simple. Imagine that you are a young person with peer pressure and hormones, enduring awkward physical changes and imminent adulthood. Even a "good" child can have a sudden desire to try a Percocet or a swig of vodka from your liquor cabinet. That young person may suddenly feel warm and fuzzy, even if he or she has no deep underlying problems or genetic tendency. Kids simply like how it feels. This is why it can be a challenge to control their desire for it once they get a taste and like it. Also, if they are watching their parents drink every night, they know it must be acceptable.

It is very helpful to engage in activities with your children and to encourage their participation in physical games and exercise. Go to a movie, a museum, a park, a library. Go roller skating, play tennis, get new bicycles, join a community gardening club. It stops them from being bored and also helps them engage in social and community activities. Working parents are short on time, but always check in on what your children are doing. Make time to spend with your family. Nothing you do at your job or for your personal benefit is as important as spending quality time with your family.

Even with all of these precautions, you may still find drugs in a teenager's bedroom or get a phone call from the police or a call from school. Remain calm, and have a conversation as soon as your loved one is sober and rested. Don't argue with the child while he or she is high. The next day, discuss ways to prevent a recurrence of the incident, and make an appointment to see the family therapist. There are support groups for parents as well, such as Al-Anon. You may feel guilty, angry, or overwhelmed, all of which are normal. Continue to be open and honest about your feelings and to communicate regularly with your family therapist about how things are going.

Remember that change takes a long time and involves hard work on everyone's part. Be thankful for whatever progress you have made, and remain hopeful. If you believe in the possibility of success, you have more chance of succeeding.

Dealing with Adult Addicts Who Do Not Live with You

Many people have an adult child or a grown sibling who is clearly struggling with alcohol or substance abuse. These people may be in their thirties or forties, largely independent, far away, or not receptive to advice from aging parents or grown friends and siblings. Perhaps they have been abusing drugs since their teen years or only recently accelerated their abuse, due to stress at home or on the job. Here are some trouble signs to pay attention to: when you hear stories about the person's addictive behavior from friends; when he or she asks you for a loan; when her house or her personal appearance starts to look messy; when he complains about problems at work; when he argues with family members or a marriage ends; when she loses a lot of weight; when he starts showing up late for everything, with a lot of excuses; when she has more outbursts of anger; when he spends more time alone. Maybe you will go for months and months without hearing from this person. Of course, this doesn't always mean your family member or friend is using anything, but if you fear for that person more than you do for others, you may reach a point where you should discuss the possibility. You want your loved one to be better, to be happy.

Be sensitive about where and when you bring up the topic. Choose a time when your loved one is not high, perhaps lunchtime during the work week. Schedule a lunch date or a breakfast, and ask, "Are you having any troubles?" or "What can I do to help you?"

Of course, the friend or the loved one must choose to help him- or herself. One of my former clients named Rob has admitted having a drinking problem, but he thinks he can train himself to simply drink less while hanging out at bars and parties near his home. He is divorced, with four teenage children, some of whom have been caught smoking dope at school. One night, a few months ago, Rob flipped his pick-up truck and broke his neck. His passenger was hardly injured, amazingly, and is still his friend, more amazingly. Rob got a citation for DUI and lost his license (and his truck) but does not yet believe that drinking is enough of a problem for him. He has discussed it with a friend or two, but most of his friends are big drinkers themselves and would hate to see Rob leave the crowd. He continues his addiction, in total denial.

Do not provide money to anyone whose sobriety is in doubt. If you feel you can approach this person's spouse, then do so. Offer to care for the person's children while he or she goes to AA meetings or to rehab. If any of your friends or adult family members are drinking or drugging, do not spend any time with them or let them in your home. If they are threatening to anyone, including themselves, you should call the police.

In some cases, you may have to let go of your relationship with an addict or an alcoholic. Do it with love, not in anger, and don't feel responsible for that person's actions. There is a limit to what you can do to help an addict who won't help himself, such as Rob. The addict might even see your separation as an example of taking control of one's life, which, in a way, provides role model behavior. By seeing this, some addicts may realize that they have the power to regain control of their lives, too. Years may pass before the person changes and you reconnect. "When you decide to get help, I'll be here for you" are some of the most helpful words you can say. In the meantime, take care of yourself and the rest of the family.

12

Healing the
Whole Family

Many doctors, psychologists, and rehabilitation professionals overlook one of the most important elements of an addict's life, which is that the entire family—not only the patient—has been virtually destroyed by the disease. The family is as lost as the addict is and, one could say, feeling the pain more acutely. After all, the addict in the family is high most of the time, messed up beyond the realm of normal life, and doesn't have to cope with reality, as everyone else does. The other family members are exhausted and, after years of damage control, are now quite dysfunctional themselves. In my opinion, treating the family is as important as treating the addict—not only because the other family members need healing, but because the sobriety of the patient depends on that family being healed.

.   .   .

Marielle's marriage started to crumble after her son, Jake, was arrested twice with marijuana. Her husband, Peter, thought that Jake would outgrow his intransigence and blamed Marielle for being too hard on their son. When Jake got addicted to heroin, Peter blamed Marielle for having made the problem worse. As his parents' marriage fell apart, Jake became a master manipulator, playing one off the other into a stereotypical triangle of persecutor, rescuer, and victim, where every member of the family traded roles.

Julie and Drew were respected professionals who had been married ten years, but they fought a lot about money. One night on the way home from work, Drew was arrested, and the cops found cocaine and marijuana in his pockets. It turned out that Julie's husband was a cocaine addict, unbeknownst to her. He entered inpatient rehab under a pretrial intervention agreement. The experience cost him his job but eventually brought the couple closer together.

George and Patsy are the toast of the neighborhood, because they give the greatest pool parties. When their teenage son, Neil, returned from rehab, they felt guilty about their heavy drinking but didn't want to stop the partying. George started to work overtime (to pay the bills for rehab), but Patsy was at a loss. She developed an insidious resentment toward her son, whom she blamed for making her feel guilty about drinking. In her passive-aggressive way, Patsy stocked the house with booze and friends, practically luring young Neil off the wagon. With George working longer hours, Patsy had lost not one but both of her drinking partners, although she would never admit to it. Neil was coping with recovery but still living with an aggressive alcoholic. His mom was not going to quit, so the family had to learn how to manage around these dynamics.

•   •   •

Addicts act out, and the rest of the family reacts. As we get used to everyone's behavior patterns, we forget that we have choices in how to react to our loved one's intoxication. Family members start to believe they must do more and more, and they doubt their ability to succeed, as time goes by, after each failed confrontation. This is when we must at least get help for ourselves.

A family cannot heal unless there is a great deal of communication, patience, and forgiveness. There is shame and guilt in some variation for every one of them, as well as plenty of anger, resentment, and confusion. Family therapy helps teach each one how to communicate effectively and helps clear the air of subconscious issues in all of the members' various relations with one another.

Dynamics vary in every family, of course, but as therapists recognize a problem in the household, we often see stereotypical roles of the codependents. This cast of characters will even re-create itself in a group of coworkers at an office or in a network of close friends, because as adults we often get into relationships that meet our unmet needs from childhood. Yours may be a family with slightly different dynamics, but in almost every case, it is a variation of the following:

The addict: As the addiction worsens, this person becomes the center of attention and a drain on the energy of every family member. Some family members will compensate and shift roles to cover for the addict, causing further tension in the family.

The hero: One person may ignore the signs that another family member is an alcoholic or an addict and may start putting on a "show" as if it's a happy family. That person is buried in shame and guilt, insisting that things are just fine.

The mascot: One sibling or child will use humor to cope with the household misery and will refuse to take it seriously. He or she avoids confrontation, out of embarrassment or anger, and enables everyone else to continue in a state of denial.

The lost child: This member will withdraw from the family dynamic, avoiding confrontation but feeling lonely, angry, and neglected.

The scapegoat: Feeling empty and shameful, this family member may act out and cause trouble to try to draw attention away from the addict or the alcoholic. This is often the middle child, as is:

The caretaker: This one is always present in the family of an addict. He or she will facilitate the addict's behavior by offering excuses and trying to keep everyone happy. Feeling fearful and inadequate, this person reacts with misguided attempts to provide love and care.

The copycat: This one will emulate the abuser, without intention, simply to reinforce familiar family patterns.

This family needs to reshape the dynamics into healthy roles and stop pointing fingers at one another, which only serves to deflect responsibility. Each of them is in pain. Therapists will help reestablish self-worth for each family member; teach clear communication, honesty, and openness; and propose simple family rules and personal goals for each person that will be supported by everyone else.

When Your Spouse Is the Identified Patient

If you are married to an alcoholic or an addict, the drama surrounding your spouse eclipses any other interest of the family. The "healthy" spouse scales back on his or her own activities and friendships, to maintain the household and perform damage control. Husbands and wives are usually the first to be in denial that their "other half" has a problem, having convinced themselves that everyone has issues of some kind. Yet in the long run, the healthier spouse will start to feel suppressed anger and depression. In addition, there is no talking reason to an addict. You need a therapist who will help you establish a support system and address your issues of codependence. Codependency in a marriage is when one partner places the needs of the spouse before his or her own. When a marriage is interrupted by a spouse's addiction, this codependency may become more acute. The "healthy" partner puts his own needs, feelings, and desires in the background in order to support and love his spouse through her recovery. He worries incessantly about her well-being, to the point where his own expression and experiences are neglected.

Codependency has the potential to stifle communication between partners. It is easy for you to fall into the pattern of not telling your spouse what you need, because everyone is busy putting the alcoholic's needs first. You may want your spouse to be more intimate or to be more generous with expressing appreciation for all you do for the family, but addiction turns people into self-centered takers. You might want to tell your spouse how unhappy you are that he is harming himself, with no thought of how it might affect those around him, but addiction causes the addict to think only of what he needs and not what he can do for others.

Marriage counseling can help you learn more about the problems you need to work on together. Yet the event that might nudge a relationship toward healthy change is the cataclysmic moment when you decide that you have had enough. The threat of losing something as beautiful as a marriage might be the very thing that causes your loved one to reexamine his behavior, to leave addiction behind, and to begin living in the solution.

All the Codependents

Family members often become codependent, which means they compensate for the addict in the family by taking on the role of someone who considers him- or herself "in control." Parents may cling to their kids, believing that extra nurturing or more money will help the addict. Spouses go out of their way to remedy bad behavior and cover up the problem of an out-of-control addict in the family. Codependency can occur in any type of relationship, including in families, friendships, and the workplace and in romantic, peer, or community environments. Codependency may also be characterized by low self-esteem, excessive compliance, control patterns, and denial. By prolonging the situation, however, we are only adding to the problem, not only for the addict, but for ourselves. Codependents become angry if their extra efforts don't change the addict's behavior. These family members need care for themselves, in addition to finding care for their loved ones.

Codependents in denial may also lack empathy for the feelings and needs of everyone else, may label others with negative characteristics, and may attempt to take care of themselves without help from anyone else. Furthermore, denial can cause a codependent person to mask his or her pain in various ways, such as anger, humor, or isolation, and express negativity or aggression in indirect and passive ways. Typically, codependent people also have difficulty recognizing the emotional and/or physical unavailability of the individuals to whom they are attracted.

A codependent relationship exists between two people; one person is recognized as being physically or psychologically addicted, such as with alcohol or drugs, and the second person is likely to be equally psychologically dependent on the addict's needs and emotions. A crucial result of treating the addict is to highlight the existing codependent behaviors of all family members involved. Once codependent people become aware of their behavior, they are encouraged to seek and accept support and help in modifying their behavior.

When Your Parent Is the Identified Patient

Children of addicts often have feelings of depression, anger, and low self-esteem and try to deflect attention by going to one of two extremes: by aiming for perfection or by lying, stealing, skipping school, and remaining withdrawn from everyone. Both are defense mechanisms that keep them emotionally detached. Without a normal childhood, the child of an addict may grow up to be insecure, unable to express feelings, and very comfortable with telling lies in order to avoid conflicts. Therapy is very helpful for adult children of alcoholics, because the problems can linger long after the parents are gone.

If your parent or parents are drinkers, you may well feel responsible for the problem. On top of coping with guilt, children are missing a positive role model who is supposed to help guide them into adulthood. In addition, younger children are quite powerless when it comes to identifying the problem and getting help. If you know someone who has young children and a personal problem with addiction, be brave and take steps to help that family. Don't be afraid to call your local Child Protective Services. We are a community. It takes a village to help and protect young friends and relatives who cannot speak for themselves. Don't worry about whether the parent will be upset if you report him or her to the authorities. You might help save lives. Often, this kind of intervention will motivate the parent to get help for his or her addiction.

Forgiveness Helps Everyone

If you are an adult child of an alcoholic, it will serve you well, first, to forgive your mother or father. It can take the children of alcoholics many years to let go of their bitterness and stop blaming themselves for their parent's condition. Even if the parent is sober now, it may take years before their children learn to trust that parent. Yet whether or not your parent ever recovers or offers you an apology for his or her addiction, at least forgive yourself. You were also a victim of your parent's disease. The National Association for Children of Alcoholics offers advice in the form of the Seven C's:

1. You didn't CAUSE your parent's addiction.
2. You can't CURE it.
3. You can't CONTROL it.
4. You can CARE for yourself by
5. COMMUNICATING your feelings.
6. Make healthy CHOICES.
7. CELEBRATE yourself.

Children of alcoholics need to learn how to think positively and lay the foundation for a happy life all their own. If your parent is still drinking or using drugs, discuss options for helping him or her by talking to siblings and friends. Join Al-Anon and hear about other experiences that might help you. Consult a therapist for your own issues in this situation, as well as to seek out options for the addicted parent.

When Your Child or Sibling Is the Patient

Susan and Mark are successful professionals who have two sons, Adam and Eric. The kids are good-looking, with above-average academic achievement. Both are athletic and participate in school sports, such as high school basketball and baseball. Adam is now a student in his second year of college, and Eric is a high school junior.

"But they are night and day," said Susan. While Adam sailed through high school without getting into trouble, Eric has been arrested twice for public drunkenness and recently was charged with a DUI manslaughter for a car accident that took the life of a young woman in another vehicle. Eric has been expelled from the school and is currently at his third rehab facility in as many years.

• • •

Be honest with everyone in the family: tell the other children that their sibling has an addiction, which is a disease, and is getting professional help. The children are worried, no matter what their age. Tell them that you are worried, too, and explain how everyone will get better with family counseling. They love their addicted sibling, just as you do, and they are fearful for him or her. Be sure to tell the siblings of the addict that they are not responsible for the happiness of anyone else in the house. Confirm that your divided attention may be a pain in the ass for a while.

Be as open as you can be with friends and grandparents and coworkers, but you need not tell them everything. Your friends or in-laws will want to help you, although some will offer unwanted advice. Some may reopen old wounds and continue in denial or even judge the way you are coping with the disease in your house. It's best to avoid people who will pass judgment that is frustrating to you.

Get Professional Help for the Family

When a parent or a child copes with the addiction of a loved one, a typical response to the seemingly out-of-control situation is denial. In denying their own codependency, these family members often have difficulty identifying their feelings or emotions; they may minimize, alter, or deny how they truly feel about any given situation, and they may mistakenly see themselves as completely unselfish and committed to the well-being of others.

Although the addict may struggle for a while after starting therapy with me, I see the family respond with an enormous sense of relief. I'm able to comfort family members with my tales of having "seen it all" and recognizing manipulation and bad behavior. Family counseling helps everyone set boundaries, take responsibility for his or her own actions and not for other people's behavior, and helps people forgive one another for the dysfunction in the house. It is also beneficial to attend community meetings such as Al-Anon, which is designed for family members to open up and share their concerns.

•   •   •

Here's what one family member said about working with me in therapy: "Our weekly family session was the most comprehensive and high-quality educational program regarding addiction we have ever experienced. After years of confusion and some seriously bad advice from other professionals, we finally were able to explore our own codependency and the vital need to attend Al-Anon routinely. With this education and support from you and Al-Anon, we have felt an enormous amount of relief and release. We no longer believe that we are responsible for our son's recovery or relapse; we no longer believe 'if we had only done this or that,' it would not have happened;

we no longer believe that 'if we just give in on this one thing, he will be all right.'"

Another parent told me, "We now know that our role is to find independence/appropriate boundaries and to love our son, but not love him to death. We can be a part of his recovery but never a willing part of his disease. In order to attain a healthy and balanced life, we, along with our son, must work our program continuously throughout our lives to give us the best chance against our relapse into codependency and his relapse into active addiction."

Here's what another parent learned: "The journey is still ongoing, but the understanding that has come as a result of the educational process has made us stronger, more balanced, and peaceful, as opposed to the emotional chaos, crises, and never-ending torment we were experiencing as we first walked in those doors when our son was admitted for heroin and alcohol addiction."

*   *   *

After your loved one completes rehab and is in recovery, he or she may seem to be a slightly different person. That's a good thing. He is starting to get to know himself in a new light. He may be more outspoken or may make new friends. Your job is to be understanding and welcome the changes, to keep track of your loved one's activities but not be distrustful. That's a fine line, I know.

Grandma, You're Drunk Again

Many of us grew up with family members who drank alcohol. Whether a flute of champagne at a birthday or a Christmas dinner or a glass of wine on a Jewish holiday, the consumption of alcoholic beverages became synonymous with family gatherings and celebrations. Perhaps we grew up hearing Grandpa's war stories while he nursed a snifter of brandy, or we helped Grandma put together scrapbooks while she sipped on her daily chardonnay. Subtle though the evidence may be, there exists a strong possibility that our grandparents, just like our parents, siblings, and some of our friends, may be alcoholics.

Alcoholism is a disease of perception that can be observed in our actions, reactions, and behaviors and in which alcohol and drugs are the solution to fear, insecurity, and discomfort. Alcoholism affects all types of people in all age ranges—the disease does not discriminate. If we have identified the disease of alcoholism as active in our behavior, it may seem easier to observe the signs of alcoholism in our loved ones. In learning that alcoholism is a family disease, family recovery is contingent on effective communication and healthy support between family members.

Grandparents, like everyone else, are susceptible to the disease of alcoholism. This might mean that they are merely physically and psychologically dependent on substances as a coping mechanism for the stresses in their lives, or it could mean that generations of family members will be forced to address and modify their behavior as a means of clearing away the wreckage caused by their excessive and destructive substance abuse.

Our parents might blame the problems they experienced in their childhoods on their parents' substance abuse—a trend we might not experience directly or be able to see because of the grandparent-grandchild relationship. Conversely, we might blame our grandparents' alcoholic behavior for the way our parents treat us—the direct result of how our upbringing can shape our experiences, perceptions, and realities and how the disease of alcoholism is perpetuated within the family system.

For alcoholics, adult children of alcoholics, and adolescent children of alcoholics, recovery begins with addressing our codependent and enabling behaviors. While the alcoholic must seek treatment and recovery in 12-step programs, such as Alcoholics Anonymous, the loved ones affected by a family member's alcoholism must also seek their own recovery in support groups, such as Al-Anon, Alateen, and Adult Children of Alcoholics (ACOA). Understanding the causes of alcoholism and how we can help our alcoholic family members, while changing ourselves, is crucial to strengthening the family and keeping it together in the face of a devastating disease.

13

Advice for Parents

You are not a bad parent if your child is an alcoholic or an addict. It is not your parenting abilities that caused your child to lose control. You love that child more than anything in the world, and there is no fault in that. In today's world, however, it seems that parents have become confused. Kids grow up faster and faster, with smartphones, social media, sophisticated TV shows, and unintelligible music. Some of you start planning for college admission before your kid enters preschool, because you think you must in order for your child to grow up and be successful. You compare your children to other people's children, assessing who is doing better than whom, and you worry about cliques and bullies and predators. You can never do enough for your kids. I get that.

However, sometimes our emotions are so strong that we become overly entangled with our children, too close to see the downside of overprotecting them. We overreact when we sense the slightest doubt of self-esteem or academic talent. We are super sensitive to birthday party invitations, honor rolls, and sports teams. We want our children to be happy and successful, and we feel better when we pursue interests on their behalf, as we believe good parents should. We struggle to protect our kids from bad influences at school, from too much TV and Internet. Some people want to turn off all media, but the truth is, kids still need to learn tools to cope with the media barrage in our current society. What they may need the most protection from, a lot of the time, is you.

Get Out of the Helicopter

I recently heard a story on the radio about an Easter egg hunt in Colorado. After several years, this town decided to cancel the annual children's event. The reason wasn't that the funding was gone, or that it was too religious or poorly attended. It was canceled because aggressive parents would swarm into the neighborhood park to make sure little Jason and little Alexis got enough Easter eggs. The parents were "helping" their children get an edge. The hunt would be over in a few seconds.

"It's the perfect metaphor for millennial children," said Ron Alsop, the author of *The Trophy Kids Grow Up*. "The parents can't stay out of their children's lives. They don't give their children enough chances to learn from hard knocks, mistakes."

With almost every alcoholic or addict I treat, I see parents who had the best of intentions but who inadvertently impeded their child's emotional growth. You want to protect your kids, but when you interfere with the natural development of self-esteem, you actually make life more difficult for them in the long run. Do you want to see your child get an Easter egg? Or is it that you don't want to feel the pain of seeing your child be disappointed? Our hearts ache for our children, whether they are troubled or not. Yet this is about your child, it is not about you.

Do Not Pass Along to Your Kids
the Disease of More

Joe's dad believes he is supporting his sixteen-year-old son by giving him every advantage. In a bargain between them, Joe gets a new BMW and a monthly allowance of several thousand dollars as long as he maintains decent grades at school and stays out of trouble with the law.

You may think that providing for your children is helpful, but it is actually the opposite. It does not bring fulfillment and happiness but only confusion and insecurity. This kind of misguided "overcompensation" from parents can establish the parameters that will create not young adults but young addicts, who then become old addicts in their lifelong search for "more." You may enjoy the good life, whether it's because of hard work or good fortune, and you deserve to do as you please, even if it is subconsciously compensating for your shortcomings or disappointments. You may deserve that new car, and you are a responsible adult. Yet when it comes to your child, you would do him or her far more good if you said no. It is easier to say yes, particularly if you can afford it, or if you feel guilty about not spending more time at home. The harder thing—and the preferable thing to do as a good parent—is to say no much more frequently than you currently do. Your children don't need cars, money, and privilege. They need a healthy foundation of family support, integrity, moral fiber, and the ability to communicate. They need to spend time with you, learning to help others and to be actively involved in community. You need to share with your children healthy ways to cope with anger, stress, frustration, and anxiety. Having your kids work for the things they want teaches them self-esteem. They learn that getting up in the morning and working at something can help them reach goals and reap the benefits of responsibility. If, instead, you shower them with things money can buy, you are setting them up for destruction. More than that, you are robbing them of the opportunity to build self-respect by learning how to do things on their own. Don't rob your children of the ability to experience success by doing it all for them.

I find great resistance from parents when I suggest that they stop the money train for their children. They think it is their "right" or their obligation as good parents. They want to be liked by their children, and they can afford to be "generous." Of course, you can do what you want, but if your child is an alcoholic or an addict, it is unconscionable that you perpetuate their disease to soothe your own insecurities. I am not judging you, because this isn't about you. Do you really want to help your child? Then do the hardest thing of all: step back.

Buying your children new cars or paying their rent will only perpetuate the drug abuse and delay their recovery. Parents often seem indignant, as if they have earned the right to spoil their children. It is as if they carry some shame of their own, and they are concealing it by piling on the stuff. I gently try to assure them that they are not doing good for their child. The fact that the kids are addicted or in a hospital should be evidence enough, but sometimes the parents are the last to admit that their golden child has a problem—or a problem that they can't fix with money. As you can imagine, patients in this kind of situation are why I recommend that the whole family enter therapy. You mean well, but, like the patient him- or herself, you and the other family members need guidance in learning new behavior that will lead everyone to authentic happiness.

Teen years are a crucible of intense experiences: dealing with changing hormones, navigating into adulthood, and coping with new emotions and responsibilities. It is a perfect storm when you introduce the opportunity to try drinking and drugging for the first time. It is up to us, as parents, to teach our children that the more they use substances, the more destruction they are causing to their brains and their future. We can't blame anyone else, such as the schools or our kids' friends who are a "bad influence." There's a reason your kid brought that "bad friend" into his circle. Don't turn a blind eye. Don't buy him a car as some type of bargain to make him act responsibly or to assuage your own guilt or other feelings.

It is a proven fact that the longer a young person puts off the first use of alcohol or drugs, the less likely that person will be to develop an addiction or any other lifelong problems. It is also widely known that parents are the most powerful influence over whether their kids will drink or use drugs. Kids don't want to lose the respect of their parents.

You don't have to abstain from your usual lifestyle, and I am not suggesting that you yourselves are addicts. Just think about it, though: do the adults in your house consume a lot of alcohol? Do you compensate for your own depression or disappointments by buying a new wardrobe or flying off on a vacation? Do you blame other people—your boss, your in-laws, your ex-spouse— for difficulties in life? Do you take a Valium when you're stressed out? Think about how you are a role model and what your children learn from the way you behave in challenging situations. It is not enough for them to do only as you say. They can't help but do as you do, but in their own ways.

Unplug and Talk

Reestablish the family meal, preferably at least four times a week. Once in a while, it is good to unplug the television, the computer, and the cell phone, to signal that family business takes precedence over everything else. Have casual, easy conversations when you are in a group; there's no need to discuss serious topics at the dinner table, such as poor grades or being grounded. Talk about things you are grateful for, and ask everyone to contribute his or her thoughts. Ask each family member to list five things he or she loves about your family. Try to avoid arguments, accusations, and threats. Teach your children how to have normal conversations that are not filled with arguments, bargaining, or threats. Remain neutral, and keep a positive attitude. If you don't have a positive attitude, then fake one. Faking optimism can often help instill it for real.

Be judicious about handing out the car keys, and be awake when your child comes home at night. Put away your prescription medications; keep track of or eliminate your liquor cabinet. Don't allow your children to go to parties if you suspect there will be alcohol or drugs. Establish ground rules if your children transgress. Some parents go too easy on their kids; they don't want to ground a child simply because they don't want a grumpy kid around the house all day. It is your house, and you are in charge. It is okay if you are not your children's friend.

Teach Gratitude

Your child has a loving parent, or two of them. Your family has much to be thankful for, no matter how little you earn or where you live or what school your child attends. There are friends and neighbors who care for the members of your family, professionals such as teachers and doctors and counselors who want to help your child grow up and be successful. Members of Alcoholics Anonymous remind one another to take "one day at a time," and that is the best way to live your lives. Show your children how wondrous it is to watch a snowstorm or how lucky you are to adopt a new cat or how to write a note to a good friend. Be grateful that you have the opportunity to eat dinner together or share home-grown tomatoes with a neighbor or that you have good health, nice neighbors, and a great coffee shop around the corner. Your world is full of good things, and if you yourself take them for granted, your child won't learn about what truly matters in life. Nice cars and nice houses are great, but they're just the "perks" of a responsible life. Honor and dignity in a young man or a young woman are qualities no one can take away from them.

Just Stay on the Course

If your kid is still using, after all of your interventions or even a stint in jail and scary medical emergencies, then try to live your lives knowing you have done everything possible. See chapter 11 on how to cope with a child who does not stay sober. When dealing with addiction and alcoholism, there is no benefit to pointing fingers or feeling responsible for the addicted person's behavior, even your own offspring. Arguing will go nowhere and will only put him or her on the defensive. Your child has a disease. Treating this particular disease is a delicate balance, and it often requires starting over again.

Find a support group such as Al-Anon or one at the local school or at your church. These are your neighbors, who maintain anonymity for your family, but who can offer a world of support that you may not find anywhere else. It is not your fault. Take care of yourself.

There is still great hope for your loved one, if only because you are there, and he or she knows it. When your loved one stops feeling comfortable in this state of addiction, he or she will see the need for change. Care for the other members of the household so that they do not feel guilty or confused. Remember that recovery is a long process, and you have at least started the journey.

•   •   •

Ever since elementary school, my daughter Katelyn was strong-willed, never wanting to do the things she was supposed to do. She threw tantrums about doing small chores around the house: taking out the garbage or cleaning her room. In second grade, she was tested at a "genius" level, and, looking back, I see that she was a kid who was not being challenged, whose mind didn't fit easily in with the rest of the crowd, although her elementary school teachers tried very hard to keep her motivated in school. She saw a psychotherapist beginning at age nine, but I don't think that had a great impact.

I noticed a difference in Katelyn when she entered sixth grade. She was in a new middle school, where she did not have a lot of friends or connections, so she was an outsider from the start. She met all of the academic "expectations" from her teachers; in fact, she loved math and probably should have been put in some kind of accelerated program, but we didn't push it at the time. She began to slide in seventh and eighth grades, and, by ninth grade, she started skipping classes.

Katelyn was always strong-headed, but she got a lot more oppositional in high school. She had extremely reactive behavior—manic highs and super-low depressions, which resembled the mood swings of bipolar disease. In retrospect, I can see that she had some symptoms of attention deficit disorder as well. She started "self-medicating" by smoking cigarettes and then pot by the time she was fourteen, which we didn't know at the time. She hung out with students who were not exactly college prep; it turns out, they were drug users, and some of them were selling drugs.

Katelyn got caught shoplifting some CDs and evidently started doing more and more drugs of all kinds: marijuana, Ecstasy, pills, you name it. Her little sister, Amanda, was nearly nine years younger and learned at an early age not to depend on her big sister. I am an educator and was considered a local expert on kids and drugs, but I was powerless to help my daughter.

My husband and I went to therapy to handle the stress of raising this angry adolescent. In his pain, my husband reacted to Katelyn's rage with his own anger. I tried to stay in a calm zone, to represent some kind of stability: my pain was on the inside, while my husband's was on the outside. One night, when Katelyn was sixteen, her rage escalated to the point where we decided to commit her to a psychiatric hospital for three weeks. We knew she had been experimenting with drugs at that point, but we didn't realize the full extent of it.

Katelyn enrolled in an alternative high school and started to get therapy, and we gave her drug tests, obviously with limited success. She had tried a number of antidepressants, such as Prozac, but they didn't really help her. She went to rehab several times in high school and relapsed every time, and then she started stealing money from us. By the time she managed to finish her senior year, she was jumpy and irritable and looked awful.

She started college but soon dropped out. She became addicted to heroin and disappeared, off and on, for the next couple of years. She would come home and try to stay clean, but everything just seemed to get worse and worse. You know how hard it is to say no to your own child? She went in and out of several more rehab facilities during her late teens and twenties. She tried methadone, and that didn't work. It seemed as though she was simply too hard-headed to commit to getting clean. Then we reached the point where we had to change the locks on our house to keep her from breaking in and stealing from us. We had to change the locks five or six times.

I wouldn't have made it if I had not found an Al-Anon group of parents who were going through similar experiences with their children. It had been too shameful to discuss Katelyn's addiction with my own mother or my friends. The members of Al-Anon helped me learn where and when to let Katelyn go. One of the mothers' stories always gave me hope through these dark times: she had a daughter in an elite private school, who eventually recovered from a terrible heroin addiction and went on to have a successful adulthood.

Addiction is not rational. It's not about a choice—the prefrontal cortex just shuts down, eliminating any ability to make good decisions. For my own survival, I knew that I had to find a way to salvage my own life. In my mind, I went through Katelyn's funeral, burying my child, and imagining how I would survive that. Every time the phone rang, I imagined that it was the police calling: "Your daughter has been in a car accident and is on life support at the hospital." I still feel the weight of that pain.

I remember my own mother having concern for me, but I told her I was determined to regain some semblance of a life beyond Katelyn. "I will survive this," I told her, as much for my own sake as for hers. My husband felt helpless and confused as well but found it hard to talk about the situation. I went to Al-Anon meetings, and so did our younger daughter, who was helped by talking with other teenagers who had addicted and alcoholic siblings.

When she was twenty-six, Katelyn knocked on our door and said, "I'm at the end of my rope. Please give me one more chance." She had been sleeping in her car. She had to go to detox for five days before she could enter rehab again. Then, while we were packing the car to drive her to the inpatient facility near Atlanta, she disappeared. A couple of hours later, she returned and crashed her car into one of our neighbor's parked cars. The police discovered that she was high on heroin and hauled her off to jail. We left her there.

After a couple of days, the judge released Katelyn on the condition that she check into the rehab center. At first, Katelyn thought it would be only a couple of weeks and then she would go back to college. But she stayed there two months, and afterward, she lived in a "halfway house" in Florida for seven months. I was so thankful that she had finally found a therapist whom she could relate to. It seemed, as though for the first time, that Katelyn didn't feel as if she was smarter than all of the doctors. It was a breakthrough for her to do something she didn't want to do, for her to give up control and trust others enough to help herself.

She got with the program. She has stayed clean for the eight years since then and is now married, with a beautiful two-year-old son. She graduated from college with a degree in finance and works as a data analyst.

I would tell any other parent in my situation that miracles do happen. Part of Katelyn's success is that she survived those bad years. As she entered her late twenties, I think she simply started to mature, and that helped her get over the need for drugs. I have also learned that kids with higher-than-average intelligence are more likely to experiment with drugs. They are often alienated from their peers and bored in school.

Katelyn goes to a psychotherapist regularly and has adjusted her antidepressant medications, but she is healthy and happy now. Miracles do happen.

*   *   *

PART FOUR

Your Life Is a Gift

14

Service to Others
and Yourself

Bruce grew up in New Jersey and went to college
during the 1960s, a wild time to be a student, the
dawn of drug experimentation for young people. Tall and
handsome, he would drink and smoke a little dope with
friends. He graduated and did very well in a business
career, moving up the corporate ladder in hospital administration. He got married, had two children, and became the
director of human resources. Bruce was revered as a boss:
selfless and smart, he was the calm in the storm when it
came to negotiating with hospital unions and charting the
changing landscape of health care. When he was divorced
in the late 1970s, Bruce moved to New York City, seeing
his son and daughter in New Jersey on a weekly basis.

Bruce's ritual as a newly single man in Manhattan was
to stop by a bar on his way home from work, which
became his home away from home, and "happy hour" on a
daily basis was considered normal for many professionals.
He met a nice woman, Marcy, and eventually moved in
with her. As the disco era and the clubs charged up in the
Big Apple, Bruce and Marcy started doing benzos and coke
and just about everything to stay up, partying at Studio 54
and the Palladium. Bruce and Marcy knew a lot of people
for scoring pretty much anything they wanted. In fact, it
wasn't too long before Bruce was making frequent trips to
Bogotá, Colombia, flying home to New York with kilos of
cocaine. Bruce was out all night, every night, the life of the
party, his quiet hipness and pockets filled with drugs a
welcome presence wherever he went. In the morning, with
no sleep, he would do some cocaine and go to work at his
office. He would do cocaine all day and go out again at
night. He lived like this for more than a decade. It is still
amazing to me that he kept going at his day job, while he
was the impresario of the night in the coke-laden days of
the 1980s.

"I had a great secretary," Bruce said. "She covered for
me when I eventually started to call in sick. I suppose
she was my enabler."

Bruce spent years addicted to cocaine but managed
to stay employed (and alive) for a long time. Then his
addiction accelerated.

"I was introduced to smoking freebase cocaine,"
Bruce recalled. "Within two years, my relationship was
falling apart, I never saw my kids, and I started calling in
sick a lot."

By that time, Bruce had twenty years' employment at
his company, where he'd somehow managed to do great

work, and where everyone loved him. He was admired by everyone: he had friends, he had money, he had professional success. He also had a totally secret life, as well as a life-threatening addiction.

"One day, I was called in to my boss's office," he recalled. "He was always so nice to me. He said, 'Bruce, are you okay? You're not showing up for work anymore. You look terrible. Do you need help?' I think he'd avoided me for months and months, and it broke his heart when he finally had to let me go."

Bruce collected severance pay and unemployment benefits for a few months and took odd jobs driving limousines around the city. He was in his forties by then, still using drugs as much as ever, and often woke up behind the wheel of his car with absolutely no memory of what he had done or where he had driven people the night before. Within a couple of months, he'd lost the chauffeur job, and his money ran out. He'd stopped bringing drugs to all of the parties, of course, and the fast crowd no longer cared about Bruce so much.

"I felt like a little sparrow under the picnic table," Bruce said, "waiting for crumbs to fall down from above."

He was eventually evicted from his apartment and lived as a squatter in an abandoned building in the Bronx for two months, scoring drugs when he could.

"My children were teenagers, living in New Jersey with their mother, and had no idea where I was. One day I was cold and hungry, living in that Bronx hellhole, and I felt an overwhelming panic. I raced outside to find a pay phone in that filthy neighborhood. I can remember dialing the operator and, at the same time, asking God for help. It was the first time I'd prayed to God. I called

my sister in L.A., collect, crying and begging her for
help."

It was the first time Bruce had asked his sister not for
money, but for help. She bought him a plane ticket to the
West Coast. Bruce packed his belongings into two
garbage bags and—filled with fear, not relief—he moved
in with his sister in Los Angeles. They made a deal: he
would stay sober, and she would let him stay at her
apartment. Bruce entered an outpatient program at a
local hospital and started to attend AA meetings.

"I guess I was lucky," he said. "I hit a hard,
humiliating bottom. When I made that call in the filthy
phone booth, I surrendered to God in that moment."

Bruce found his new home in an AA group in North
Hollywood. It was like happy hour at his old bar in
Manhattan, only without the drinking and the fistfights.

"But we laughed," he said. "That kept me coming
back." Bruce sent out hundreds of resumes and finally
found a job cleaning studio rental trucks. Eventually he
got work selling X-rated movies to video stores, which led
to his starting his own business buying and selling videos.
But it got old. Bruce went back to graduate school at
night, and after two years earned a master's degree in
marriage and family therapy. He interned at a nonprofit
rehabilitation center and worked at a homeless shelter. I
met Bruce when he applied to be program director at our
treatment center, and I have learned so much from him.

•   •   •

Running a rehab facility is not an easy job, as you might imagine. We negotiate with judges and lawyers, doctors and parents,
never mind the patients. We have a collection of distinctive and
unbalanced personalities and a wide variety of addictions and

psychological conditions. These people depend on Bruce—and our other counselors—to learn how to stabilize their bodies and their emotions and to learn basic self-management skills and personal responsibility. Bruce has an amazing, innate talent for reaching people who are, as he once was, beyond desperate, yet still resistant to change.

Now, not all recovered addicts were meant to work as addiction counselors. Yet recent studies show that volunteering in some way can help you better recover from addiction and even prevent addictive behaviors in the first place. High school students and young adults were part of a University of Missouri study that showed that becoming involved in community efforts, volunteering in organizations such as Meals on Wheels, coaching, or mentoring other youngsters were activities that protected adolescents from engaging in risky behavior, such as drinking and smoking marijuana.

"Pro-social behaviors are good for society and communities, but they are also a marker of moral development," said Professor Gustavo Carlo, the author of the study. "There is a tendency for youths to take part in risky behaviors if they are not engaged in positive, structured activities. If we can develop programs that foster pro-social behaviors, we know the programs will decrease the likelihood that adolescents will use substances in adulthood."

Major studies published by Americorps confirmed that volunteering just two hours a week provided significant health benefits for all ages, including lower rates of depression and anxiety.

"Civic engagement and volunteering are the new hybrid health club for the 21st century, and it's free to join," said Thomas Sander of Harvard University. *Helping Out* magazine published a survey that revealed how people felt after volunteering:

"I have a sense of satisfaction from seeing the results."
    (97 percent)

"I really enjoy it." (96 percent)

"It gives me a sense of personal achievement." (88 percent)

"I meet people and make friends." (86 percent)

"It gives me the chance to do things that I am good at."
   (83 percent)

To use my own words, helping other people will save your fucking life. I work with others in order to stay on track myself. It's not altruistic. It took me a long time to figure out that for me, my spirituality and self-fulfillment are manifested in helping another addict. It feels absolutely terrific to make inroads with a new addict, to help stop him or her from getting loaded, even for one day. Addicts and alcoholics are great at helping other addicts and alcoholics, because we have been to that hell and have crawled our way back.

I have many clients who are in the media—actors, sports stars, society figures. In some instances, the whole world learns about their addictions through the media. A big part of what I teach these patients is, if they want their careers to grow, they must remain sober. These clients can be examples to others, can be of service. I use myself as an example of addiction on TV interview programs, in order to educate others. I want to reach as many struggling addicts as I can, so I talk about how I am a convicted felon. I was scared straight by the prospect of prison and then discovered a far better version of myself when I got sober.

Shit Normies Say to 12-Steppers

I love the YouTube videos by Frankie Norstad. More artists in recovery should produce stuff like this.

"So, you can't have just one?"

"It's that boy you were dating: he's the problem."

"God, your life must be boring."

"It's all about self-control."

"I've seen drug addicts. You're not an addict."

"Do you really think talking about it helps?"

"You, in a room with a bunch of bikers?"

"What about just saying no, have you tried that?"

"So, you can be our designated driver now, right?"

"Your father had a problem; you never had a problem."

"What about Christmas or Fourth of July?"

"Do you talk about me at meetings?"

"You look really healthy."

"So, can you still have sex?"

"What about when you get married?"

"Do you think I have a problem?"

"Alcohol's not a drug!"

"I am more of an addict than you are, and I am not an addict."

"I stopped drinking, too. For like three weeks."

"I'd invite you, but you probably wouldn't have any fun."

"Do you miss it?"

"I think my cousin's girlfriend has a problem. Could you talk to her?"

"So, what, you believe in Jesus now?"

"What do you do for fun?"

"You can still eat rum balls, right?"

There are many ways you can find an outlet for helping others. I have a friend who is an attorney in Connecticut. Robert was arrested for a DUI and had his law license suspended for several months. He went to rehab for "pretrial intervention" as part of a plea agreement, which is a common scenario. During his rehab, he was contacted by another lawyer from an organization called Lawyers Helping Lawyers. Robert was amazed to discover that there was an underground network of attorneys who were in recovery and who offered support for others like them who suffered from addiction. Robert now volunteers his time with this organization and helps other lawyers regain their footing—personally and professionally—in recovering from addiction and alcoholism.

I get my energy and motivation to treat addicts when they break down and start to get in touch with their true feelings. I'm proud to be a part of that process; I feel honored that the clients are willing to be so emotional with me. That's my moment of spirituality, because nothing feels more powerful than that connection. For me, fulfillment is found in those moments.

Helping others can be as simple as using your newly found sobriety to focus on your children, your spouse, or your aging parents. You may join a literacy organization or become a candy striper at your local hospital. Volunteering helps bring you out of yourself, and you are grateful for your own blessings when you see some of the frightening obstacles faced by others in your community. When I first started to counsel addicts, I did it for selfish reasons and not for altruism. I did it to save my fucking life. It kept me on track in my own sobriety. Then mentoring other young people started to seep into my soul. It became spiritual work for me. If at first you don't feel that euphoria, keep at it. It forces you to work through fears and ego and will allow you to open doors to find your passion.

* * *

Bruce has been sober now for more than twenty-five years and has helped countless addicts at the Hills and other rehab centers. He looks back at his years as a cocaine addict and shakes his head.

"I had to go through that experience in order to get the message," he recalls. "No one is going to change if they are too comfortable. I got pretty uncomfortable in that unheated Bronx apartment. I've learned that I have a talent for helping a variety of different personalities work through their resistance. It feels empowering, even though it can be stressful at times. When I was on drugs, I had lost a piece of myself. This is the authentic me."

· · ·

When you become sober, it can be a shock to learn that the world is not all about you. You will feel better if you share your time with someone who needs whatever small part of your day you have to offer. You spent a lot of your life being high. Now, why not spend a little time being here?

Volunteering: There Is a Perfect Fit for You

Here are a few ideas to help you find the right place to volunteer your time:

- Help children learn and grow. Become a Big Brother or a Big Sister or a camp counselor, or volunteer for an after-school sports program.
- Be a holiday helper. Go to a homeless shelter to help serve Thanksgiving dinner or distribute toys to kids. Ask at your church or place of worship to learn what project you might join.
- Play with kittens and puppies. Most animal shelters depend on volunteers to keep the homeless pets healthy. Most shelters require a minimum age of fourteen for volunteers.
- Help injured veterans. Join organizations, such as Canines for Veterans or the Mission Continues or your local VA hospital, that provide assistance for disabled soldiers.
- Help save the planet. Join an environmental group and help with river or wetlands preservation,

cleaning parks, or working as a volunteer at a county
or state park.

- Get behind a healthy cause. You may know someone
  who has cancer, HIV, or diabetes, ailments from
  which those patients will never recover. Why not
  join a hospital or a group that raises money for
  research, organizes walkathons, delivers meals, or
  offers help to people with an illness?

15

The Grateful Life

When you finally learn that you don't need drugs and alcohol to be happy, this realization can feel euphoric in itself. Without addiction and shame, you will take new pleasure in everyday activities and start to feel thankful that you can now appreciate them for what they are: simple joys of everyday life. You were once desperate, but now you have learned honesty, empathy, and compassion. You have stopped hurting yourself, stopped being a victim in your own life. Isn't that incredible? Show your gratitude by living a grateful life.

Let your true self shine through to others, without fear. You are a good person, and by being good to yourself, you will help others. This comes naturally when you start to live each day filled with thankfulness for being here. You survived a lot of shit. Good for you! No time for regrets. Treat yourself like the valuable, caring person that you are. Love yourself, and make a commitment to honor your own life now, just for your own sake. Indulge in positive activities—cook a romantic dinner, go for a bike ride, see a movie. Forgive your friend or your children when they have a bad day. Be grateful that they are in your life. Opening your heart will quiet your mind and nourish your spirit. Say a prayer of thanks every day.

Gratitude is a choice we make, and I can't think why any of us would not choose to be grateful. The only other option is entitlement, and we have already learned the terrible places that can lead to. Gratitude is a gift that you give yourself, because it aligns your happiness. Your life is a mirror. Live the life you want to see, because the way you think will create your tomorrows.

Greet every day with a smile. Love your body, and let the world know you are happy to be here. Watch your life become more loving, healthy, and prosperous. Choose to live a grateful life, every day.

Find Your Passion and Your Authentic Self

One of my clients, Rebecca, was a high-powered publicist in Hollywood. I originally met her through other clients who were her friends. Rebecca's business is a tough one: the money and the luxurious lifestyle are bountiful, but so are the best drugs. One day, she admitted to me that she herself was addicted to cocaine. She started therapy with me and began going to AA meetings. It took a couple of years for her to get sober, which is not surprising, considering that she was in the movie business. After she was in recovery for about nine years, at the pinnacle of her career, she decided that she didn't want to be a Hollywood publicist anymore. She quit her job and studied to obtain a therapist's license. Now she owns a sober living house and manages several recovery projects in L.A., where there is a huge need in the community.

. . .

My story was similar. I realized that for me to be my authentic self, I had to go to graduate school. Yet I had barely managed to get through college. My disease was still telling me, "You are too stupid to go to graduate school." So here's what I replied: "Fuck you, beast." It was not easy. It took every ounce of effort for me to focus, and being a student was, as it always was, totally uncomfortable for me. It took me about seven years to get my master's and my doctorate in psychology. That was the hardest thing I ever had to do. Well, actually, getting sober was harder, but committing to anything with your heart and soul takes a lot of work. The first thing I committed to was my sobriety; the second most difficult commitment was to my career and earning that degree. The third major commitment I made was to my marriage and children. I learned that only when you are 100 percent committed will you find true happiness. After getting my degree, of course, I had to take the state exam to get my therapist's license. I failed the exam twice. I didn't give up, even though the bad crazy me was still whispering in my ear: "You can't pass that exam!" I picked up learning tools along the way and maintained my confidence, shaking off the negative thoughts from the beast. I was aware of that part of the disease by now, trying to sabotage me with negative thought patterns. I finally passed the exam on my third try.

Once you recover from addiction or alcoholism and overcome the fear of making commitments, you learn what it is to truly live. You become what you were meant to be. How many times have you heard someone tell you that you have "potential"? Aren't you tired of hearing that? I was. When you make a true commitment to something, your potential is fully realized, and people will stop saying that to you.

Like Rebecca, I found my passion in helping others, which also helps keep me sober. That is why we are all here on this planet. Passion for what you do is the key to your fulfillment and happiness. An artist or a writer who claims that drugs and alcohol "make him more creative" is full of shit. Working with other artists, being of service to your passion and your community, and sharing with others: that's what will make you more creative.

Figure out how you can give back to others in a way that fuels your passion. Because each of us is confined to our own skin, we must be honest with ourselves, about how we feel, and about what our truth is. We need to remove the ego and our fears in order to reach the truth. Connecting with your higher power—whatever that is—can bring moments of peace and contentment. You are in a direct line with your heart, in touch with humility. Keep that connection to find contentment. I know, it is easier said than done. Yet if you are true to what you really love, you will be happy. Be your authentic self, one day at a time.

When you are sober, a therapist can then help you identify your authentic self, the person you were truly meant to be. He or she will help you see the connections between your heart's desire and actual opportunities in the real world. You will have no fear, and your ego will step aside to let your true identity out. This is the part of you who can express your feelings with no bullshit, who has no passive-aggressiveness toward situations. When you know what your limitations are, you have more power over your life.

Writer and philosopher Eckhart Tolle spent many years in a deep suicidal depression. He had a psychic shift when he was twenty-nine and identified this shift as something he should share with others. Tolle realized after his breakthrough that his path was to teach other people so that they could improve their own lives. He drew on resources such as the Bible and Zen Buddhism, and his books *The Power of Now* and *A New Earth* have been huge best-sellers. Tolle has helped millions awaken to their lives' purpose. These themes ring a familiar "bell" for people who are in Alcoholics Anonymous, because many of Tolle's teachings are found in the AA "Big Book" of the 12 steps.

First, Tolle says, live in the present moment, and don't worry about the things in the past or that await in the future. The human ego is a distraction that causes us to worry about things we can't control.

Second, he says, believe in self-realization. Only when we understand ourselves will we enjoy our happiness. This understanding helps us realize that each of us has a place in the world, and each of us is important because it is our destiny to see that the universe continues to unfold.

Tolle also encourages using the Bible for what it is worth to you. Just as AA suggests, there are spiritual truths in the Bible, as well as other messages that have not aged as well. When you arrive at self-awareness, you will be able to distinguish between what's meaningful and what is not and will still benefit from the parts that help you.

Tolle reminds us that those who need "things" are not yet enlightened. Needing things is a sign that you believe in the future more than in the present moment. You are vulnerable, and you will make compromises. The present holds everything we need to find happiness. We shouldn't look at the present as a "means to an end," because in the moment is where self-realization will occur. Wanting to have some nice things is okay. When you need to have those things, you are in trouble.

We have also learned reactions that Tolle calls "pain-body attacks." We have been conditioned to think and act in certain ways, and this embedded behavior can cause us harm. By understanding these feelings, we gain more self-awareness and become able to control them.

Tolle also counsels us, "Do not fight what is." We cause our own pain when we fight against events in our lives. This resistance against "what is" causes a repeating cycle of sadness and stress. Simply accepting "what is" takes us all to a higher level and gives us the strength to achieve great things.

There You Are

Another writer who hits a chord about the power of mindfulness is Jon Kabat-Zinn. He identifies a program calls mindfulness-based stress reduction (MBSR) and has started programs around the country for schoolchildren to engage in this mind-set at a young age. He also designed programs called mindfulness-based relapse prevention (MBRP).

Kabat-Zinn compares mindfulness to thinking about your body as a guesthouse, where you invite inside all of your feelings and thoughts, and, rather than rejecting them, you enjoy their presence as if they were your friends. Practicing not to think about the past or the future and accepting the presence of all of your thoughts—even if they are negative—can decrease your stress. He cites Buddhist teachings about how mindfulness is a sense of being nonjudgmental of your current mental state, your thoughts, even physical pain, and explains how you should merely observe them as if from afar. When a thought from the past enters your mental imagery, let it go. Students in his program shift their thinking from the right prefrontal cortex (the home of anxiety and depression) to the left prefrontal cortex (the brain's center of enjoyment and happiness). His program has been shown to decrease not only stress, but disease and illness.

MBRP has proved to result in better coping skills and resistance to physical pain. Another study using MRI showed that this mindfulness program increased the number of brain cells in areas vital to learning, memory, and emotions. Learning mindfulness can change your brain.

In terms of relapse prevention, such mindfulness practices have helped former addicts develop awareness of their internal reactions to triggers. You can learn how to experience these feelings with a detachment that enables you to control your reactions and stay on course in recovery. Meditation practices, as well as yoga, can be enjoyable ways to learn how to relax and let go of troublesome thoughts. There are a variety of "schools of thought" and variations on meditation and yoga, and you might have a pretty good time trying them all, to see if one of them works for you.

If This Sick Dope Fiend Can Make It, So Can You

You are different, no doubt about it. You have been living, perhaps for a long time, through the foggy windows of addiction that prevented you from seeing life clearly and from being heard and understood by others. You've been bumping into walls and telling yourself that everything is fine. It is a shock to remove that barrier, finally walk through a door, and encounter the noisy, difficult world of reality. At the same time that you contend with the brutal light of day, you must learn new behavior and patterns of thinking and leave behind the old comfortable patterns that were ruining your life. No one has the magic answer to what will bring you fulfillment and happiness. Even "normies" who don't have addiction problems still confront plenty of challenges in living their daily lives and finding fulfillment. You must learn to live your life, as everyone else must.

Viktor Frankl, the concentration camp survivor, said, "Between stimulus and response there is a space. In that space is our power to choose our response. In our response lies our growth and our freedom." As an addict or an alcoholic, you and I were not free. We were isolated, depressed, and confused. I am an open book now, as you will soon be, and that brings a liberating sense of wholeness and authenticity.

Staying sober does not mean you won't have disappointments and challenges in your life. Not everyone ends up with the perfect career and family, and even if he does, his life may still be difficult. Yet that is why we were put here: to learn from one another, to share, and then move on. This world is plenty good enough for you and me. Stand up and start exploring it, with an open mind and an open heart. Yes, we need to find jobs that are hopefully enjoyable. This is part of being a responsible member of the community. Yet you will also meet people who love you, just the way you are, and you will be supported by your global village of recovering addicts and alcoholics who are here to lend you a hand.

It's Good to Be Good Crazy

I will never be as successful as my father was or even as my brother and sisters are. I will never be able to have a casual drink or start a healthy new career in the movie business. I live next door to a landscape of fortune and fame, such as will never be known by me, but I don't define myself by other people. In the years since, I have come to learn that all that glitters is not gold, and I wouldn't trade my life with any of those people. I may have some regrets, particularly about me and my dad, but I don't define myself by those, either.

I am dedicated to what I do, and I have come to know some amazing people, whom I never would have met if I hadn't gotten sober. That includes my wife, Gabrielle, with whom I now have three beautiful children. I may have challenges in my life from time to time, but so does everyone. I am comfortable in my own skin, and I know I am who I was meant to be. For some of us, it takes months and years of work to become our authentic selves. For many of us, we have become more self-aware and fulfilled than people who never had a problem with addiction in the first place. Is it possible we can look at this "curse" and give thanks that it somehow forced us to wake up and become better people? Better people not only in terms of how we used to be, but compared to many others who never had to meet challenges, and whose minds are still closed. By confronting your emotional pain and learning how to cope with it, you are more self-aware than most other people in the world.

I call it good crazy. Now that we're sober, we don't really want to be "normal." We're still offbeat, street-smart, foul-mouthed, or straightlaced, the best musicians and artists, the company CEOs, and funkiest suburban moms. I still want to break some rules and surprise people. You and I have been through hell. Let's keep the good crazy going, because no matter what your age, life holds great promise for you now.

Resources

Emergency Assistance

If you or a loved one needs medical assistance, or if you fear someone is going to get hurt, call 911 or ask someone nearby to make the call.

If you would like someone to talk to about yourself or a loved one, phone centers are open 24 hours a day, 7 days a week. A counselor who can answer your immediate questions and help you find local therapists or group meetings will take your phone call.

The Hills Treatment Center
1-800-724-8207
www.thehillscenter.com

Finding Professional Help/Rehab/Therapists Who Specialize in Alcoholism and Addiction

Chapter 7, "Shedding the Shame and Guilt," outlines in more detail how to choose the right kind of psychotherapist or rehab center for your situation. There are many directories on the Internet and in phone directories for local addiction counseling and rehab centers. Ask your personal physician or local health-care facility or consult a friend who may have good local referrals. Ask your local hospital or school counselors, or contact a national resource, such as:

> National Alcoholism and Substance Abuse Information Center
> 1-800-784-6776
> www.addictioncareoptions.com
>
> National Council on Alcoholism and Drug Dependence
> 1-800-NCACALL
> www.ncadd.org

You can also find a good therapist, rehab counseling, and group meetings at one of the health or support organizations, such as those listed below. Naturally, we at the Hills can help you locate a good facility, no matter where you live. Treatment centers often refer patients to places closer to their homes and work. We really want you to get effective help.

If you visit the website for the Hills Center at www.thehills center.com, you will find more information about the following issues on the Drug Rehab Guide (www.thehillscenter.com/drug-rehab):

Family Involvement
- Types of Family Therapy Approaches for Drug Treatment
- Sending a Family Member to Alcohol Rehab
- Dealing with a Family Member in Treatment
- Helping a Family Member
- What If the Addict Does Not Want Help?
- Common Concerns for Parents of Drug Addicts
- Treatment Options for Adolescents
- Will We Be Allowed to Visit Our Family Member?
- What Is Al-Anon?
- What Is Codependency?

Specific Drugs
- Cocaine Rehab
- What to Expect
- Marijuana Rehab
- Heroin Rehab
- OxyContin Rehab
- Vicodin Rehab
- Methamphetamine Rehab
- Alcohol Rehab
- Benzodiazepine Rehab
- Crack Rehab
- Prescription Drug Dependency

Treatment Facilities
- Types of Treatment
- Does Treatment Differ Depending on the Type of Dependency?
- Luxury Rehab
- Executive Rehabs
- Addiction Treatment
- Facilities for Men
- Facilities for Women
- Residential Programs
- Private Drug Rehabilitation Programs
- Celebrity Rehab
- Holistic Recovery Information
- Private Programs
- What Is Holistic Drug Rehab?
- What Is the Difference between Residential, Inpatient, and Outpatient?

- What is the Difference between Treatment and Rehab?
- Adolescent Rehab
- Information for Gays and Lesbians Entering a Program
- HIV and AIDS Patients
- Programs for Individuals with Co-Occurring Disorders
- Dual-Diagnosis Treatment Centers
- Drug Detox

Before Entering Rehab

- Drug Rehab
- How Do I Decide Which Rehabilitation Program to Go To?
- Is It the Right Decision?
- Will I Be Allowed to Use the Phone at the Facility?
- Can We Tour Facilities before Making a Decision?
- Is There a Process of Getting into a Facility? If so, What Is It?
- What Does a Treatment Center's Accreditations and Certifications Mean? Is This Important?
- How Effective Is It?
- What Is the Environment at a Program Like?
- Do I Have to Go? Can I Just Do It on My Own?
- How Long Do Programs Last?
- How Can I Find the Best Place?
- What Is It Like? What Goes on There?
- Will I Be Cured after Going through a Program?
- Why Do I Need a Rehabilitation Program?
- How Can I Go to Rehab If I Have Obligations with Work or School?
- How Do I Know the Level of Care I Need in Drug Rehab?
- Is There Someone Who Can Assess Me before I Choose a Program?

- Do I Need to Detox before I Enter a Treatment Facility?
- Can I Bring My Prescription Medication to Rehab?

Financial Issues

- Is Treatment Worth Its Cost?
- How Much Do Programs Cost?
- Are There Any Free Options?
- Will My Insurance Cover Treatment?
- What Specifically Am I Paying For?
- How Can the Government Help Me Pay?
- How Can I Enter a Treatment Center on a Budget?
- What Are the Costs of Aftercare Support Programs?
- Financing the Cost of Rehab
- Refund Policy

Legal Issues

- Can I Go to Treatment Instead of Jail?
- Does Rehab Help with Work or Legal Issues?
- Is Rehab Like Jail?
- Drug Treatment in Jails and Prisons
- Illegal Activities
- How Can Drug Rehab Affect My Court Case?
- Can a Judge Order Me to Attend Rehab?
- Minors and Drugs
- What Are the Consequences of Minor in Possession (MIP) Charges?
- The Three Strikes Law and Drugs
- Can I Enter a Drug Rehabilitation Facility with Open Charges?

After Drug Rehab
- What to Do After
- Leaving a Program
- Aftercare
- I Am Out of Treatment… Now What? What Is Life Like After?
- What Is a Sober Living?
- What Is the Difference between a Sober Living and a Halfway House?
- 12-Step Programs
- Benefits of Aftercare
- What to Expect in Early Recovery
- Expanding Your Sober Network
- What Is a Sponsor and How Do I Get One?
- What Happens If I Relapse?

Support Groups

Alcoholics Anonymous
   www.aa.org
Narcotics Anonymous
   www.na.org
Al-Anon and Alateen
   www.al-anon.alateen.org

The following websites offer podcasts and brochures that outline their programs, and they also put you in contact with local meetings and venues.

National Alliance on Mental Illness
   www.nami.org
   (800) 950-6264

Families Anonymous
   1-800-736-9805
   familiesanonymous.org

National Institute on Drug Abuse
   1-800-662-HELP
   www.drugabuse.gov

Substance Abuse and Mental Health Services Administration
   www.samhsa.gov

National Depressive and Manic Depressive Association
   www.ndmda.org
   (800) 826-3632

National Foundation for Depressive Illness, Inc.
   www.depression.org
   (800) 239-1265

Dual Recovery Anonymous (DRA)
   www.dualrecovery.org
   (888) 869-9230

National Council on Alcoholism and Drug Dependence, Inc.
   www.ncadd.org
   1-800 NCA-CALL

Helpful Blogs and Websites for Recovering Addicts and Alcoholics

It is amazing to see the growth of social networks that provide patient-to-patient support in blogs and websites, on Facebook and Twitter. People share their stories and answer questions, pretty much twenty-four hours a day, seven days a week, from all around the globe. These, as well as live chat rooms on many of the sites listed previously, are only a few of the resources you will find on the web.

www.sexualrecovery.com/blog

www.naonlinerecovery.org/subpage5.html

www.reddit.com/r/REDDITORSINRECOVERY
www.reddit.com/r/stopdrinking
www.anonymousone.com

Great Books for Those in Recovery and Their Families

Everywhere You Go, There You Are by Jon Kabat-Zinn (Hyperion, 1994)

The Power of Now by Eckhart Tolle (New World, 2004)

Families on the Fault Line by Lillian B. Rubin (Harper, 1994)

I Didn't Ask to Be in This Family: Sibling Relationships and How They Shape Adult Behavior and Dependencies by Abraham J. Twerski, M.D., and Charles M. Schulz (Holt, 1996)

Addictive Thinking: Understanding Self-Deception by Abraham J. Twerski, M.D. (Hazelden, 1997)

The Selfish Brain: Learning from Addiction by Robert L Dupont, M.D. (Hazelden, 2000)

It Will Never Happen to Me: Growing Up with Addiction as Youngsters, Adolescents, Adults by Claudia Black (Ballantine, 1987)

Another Chance: Hope and Health for the Alcoholic Family by Sharon Wegscheider-Cruse (Science & Behavior, 1989)

Adult Children of Alcoholics by Janet G. Woititz (HCI, 1990)

Addict in the Family: Stories of Loss, Hope, and Recovery by Beverly Conyers (Hazelden, 2003)

One Breath at a Time: Buddhism and the Twelve Steps by Kevin Griffin (Rodale, 2004)

Mindfulness and the 12 Steps: Living Recovery in the Present Moment by Therese Jacobs-Stewart (Hazelden, 2010)

Recovery—The Sacred Art: The Twelve Steps as Spiritual Practice by Rami Shapiro (Spiritual Paths, 2009)

Gratitude: A Way of Life by Louise L. Hay (Hay House, 1996)

Codependent No More by Melody Beattie (Hazelden, 1987)

The Mindfulness Revolution, edited by Barry Boyce (Shambhala, 2011)

Facing Love Addiction: Giving Yourself the Power to Change the Way You Love by Pia Mellody (Harper, 1992)

Mobile Apps to Help Your Recovery

Use your smartphone to keep these tools handy! Some software downloads are free of charge (such as the meeting locators), others charge a one-time fee, between one and five dollars.

Sponsor Support, Optimized Telecom Inc.

Steps Away—Locate Worldwide 12 Steps Meetings, DBJ Apps

MORE Field Guide to Life, Hazelden

12 Steps AA Companion, Dean Huff

AA Big Book and More, Rob Laltrello

Friend of Bill, Falesafe Consulting, Inc.

Joe & Charlie—AA, Robert Keathley

One Day at a Time—AA, Robert Keathley

Friend of Jimmy—NA, Falesafe Consulting, Inc.

Index

abstinence-violation effect, 166
Adderall, 43
addiction
  alcoholism, 36–37
  to "bath salts," 41–42
  as "beast," 48–49
  behavioral, 44–47, 53–54,
    90–96
  characteristics of, 2–3
  to cocaine, 27–28, 39–40,
    52–53, 54–55
  as defense mechanism, 56
  defined, 6
  delaying use of drugs and
    alcohol, 220
  denial of, 59–60, 208–209
  to depressants, 44
  effect of, on families, 177–187
    (See also families)
  fallback addictions, 90–96
  genetics and, 52–55
  to heroin, 24, 38–39
  to marijuana, 37–38

  to methamphetamine,
    40–41
  nature of, 4–5
  negative reinforcement of,
    49–50
  obsessive thinking and, 51–52
  to painkillers, 42–43
  personality and, 56–59
  prevalence of, 5, 19, 27–28,
    36–37, 38–39, 41, 42–43,
    45, 46
  to stimulants, 43
  See also intervention; therapy;
    treatment
adult addicts, intervention for,
  201–202
Adult Children of Alcoholics
  (ACOA), 215
Al-Anon, 200, 210, 212, 215
Alateen, 114–115, 215
Alcoholics Anonymous
  "Big Book," 245
  description of, 106–114

259

Alcoholics Anonymous
(continued)
sponsors, 117
See also 12-step programs;
worksheets, for 12 steps
alcohol use. See addiction;
12-step programs
Alsop, Ron, 217
Americorps, 235
anger, "dry drunk" behavior and,
94–96
Antabuse, 71
antidepressants, 68, 69–70
anxiety, addiction and, 68–70
Ativan, 44
authentic self, finding, 242–246

bars, avoiding, 173
"bath salts," 41–42
"beast," addiction as, 48–49
behavioral addiction
compulsive behavior as
fallback addiction, 90–94
"dry drunk," 94–96
gambling addiction, 46–47
Internet addiction, 96
love addiction, 44
pornography addiction, 45
sex addiction, 45
symptoms of, 53–54
video game addiction, 46
Belushi, John, 30, 56
benzodiazepines, 44
"Big Book" (Alcoholics
Anonymous), 245

binge drinking, 36–37
brain
addiction withdrawal and,
70–73
anxiety and, 68–70
depression and, 67–68
development of, 6–7
frontal lobe development of,
62–67
neurotransmitters, 61–62
"pleasure pathway" of, 55
buprenorphone, 71
bupropion, 71

Carlo, Gustavo, 235
Child Protection Services, 209
cocaine
addiction to, 39–40, 52–53
prevalence of, in 1970s, 27–28
self-medicating with, 54–55
codependency
characteristics of, 85–86, 205,
207, 208–209
denial and, 59–60, 208–209
relapse and, 164–165
Columbia University, 10
communicating
with addicts, 185–187, 207
by parents, 220–221
companions, sober communal
programs and, 119
compulsive behavior. See
behavioral addiction
"crack" cocaine, 39–40
"crank," 40

"crystal meth" ("crystal"), 40
cutting, 92–93

Davis, Jorja
  on addiction treatment, 57,
    66, 77–78, 81–82
  on repetitive actions as
    therapeutic, 102–103
defense, addiction as, 56
Demerol, 42–43
denial, addiction and, 59–60,
    208–209. See also
    codependency
depressants, addiction to, 44
depression, brain's role in
    addiction, 67–68
detoxification, determining need
    for, 71–72
disclosure, to therapists,
    184–185
"Disease of More," 7, 9, 50,
    86–89, 101–103, 218–220
disulfiram, 71
Dobbs, David, 64
Dolophione, 71
dopamine, 61–62
Downey, Robert, Jr., 161
"dry drunk," 94–96

eating disorders, 93
Ebert, Roger, 119–120, 161
Encounter (drug rehabilitation
    program), 26–27
"executive" functions, brain
    and, 63

Facing Love Addiction (Mellody),
    91
fallback addictions
  compulsive behavior, 90–94
    (See also behavioral
    addiction)
  "dry drunk," 94–96
families, 203–215
  children/siblings as addicts,
    210–211
  codependency of, 85–86,
    164–165, 205, 207,
    208–209
  effect of addiction on,
    203–206
  family contracts, 198–199
  forgiveness of, 210
  grandparents as addicts,
    213–215
  parents as addicts, 209
  professional help for whole
    family, 212–215
  spouse as addict, 206–208
  See also intervention; parents;
    relationships
Farley, Chris, 56, 88–89
fear, of relapse, 169
feelings, expression of, 27, 57–58
financial issues
  cost of rehabilitation, 193
  parents' decision to support
    addicted children, 195–199
  wealth and addiction ("Disease
    of More"), 7, 9, 50, 86–89,
    101–103, 218–220

forgiveness, 210
Frankl, Viktor, 57, 104,
    247–248
Freud, Sigmund, 51
frontal lobe, development of,
    62–67. *See also* brain

gambling addiction, 46–47
genetics, addiction and, 52–55
goals
    importance of, 8
    for treatment, 79, 81–82
grandparents, as addicts,
    213–215
gratitude, 241–249
    as choice, 241–242
    finding passion and authentic
        self, 242–246
    importance of, 103–104
    mindfulness and, 246–247
    parents' role in, 221–222
    staying sober and, 247–249
guilt
    gratitude instead of,
        103–104
    issues of, 97–100
    writing in journals to
        overcome, 100–101

Harvard University, 235
"hash," 37
Heart of Recovery, 118
Helping Out, 235
Hendrix, Jimi, 39, 56
heroin, addiction to, 24, 38–39

Hills Treatment Center, 77–89
    clients of, 234–235
    codependency issues and,
        85–86
    creation of, 33
    programs, 35
    recovery program types, 77–84
    relapse issues and, 86–89
    12-step program worksheets,
        122
humility, 111–112

"ice," 40
id, 51
inpatient rehabilitation,
    191–194. *See also* therapy;
    treatment
insomnia, 169–172
instant gratification, addiction
    and, 48–49
intake interviews, with
    therapists, 184–185
Internet, addiction to, 96
intervention, 177–202
    addicts' effect on family,
        177–187
    adult addicts and, 201–202
    arranging to intervene,
        187–191
    awareness and, 181–182
    finding therapist for, 182–185
    inpatient rehabilitation,
        191–194
    outpatient rehabilitation, 191
    to protect young children, 209

role modeling for addicts,
199–201
support for addicts and,
195–199
wilderness therapy, 194–195

journals, 100–101
Jung, Karl, 51–52

Kabat-Zinn, Jon, 246–247
Klonopin, 44
Kordite, 13

LAAM, 71
Last Call, 117–118
Lawyers Helping Lawyers,
237–238
learning disabilities, addiction
and, 14
"living in the moment," 167
love addiction, 44, 90–91

marijuana, addiction to, 37–38
Marlatt, Alan, 166
Martin, Mary, 18
Max's Kansas City (New York
City), 20
McGovern, George, 67
McGovern, Terry, 67
medication
for addiction withdrawal, 70–73
antidepressants, 68, 69–70
medical supervision during
rehabilitation, 192
for sleep, 170–171

melatonin, 170–171
Mellody, Pia, 91
mental health
addiction symptoms and,
53, 84
anxiety, 68–70
depression, 67–68
methadone, 71
methamphetamine, addiction to,
40–42
Millman, Robert B., 56
mindfulness
mindfulness-based relapse
prevention (MBRP),
246–247
SOBER (Stop, Observe,
Breathe, Expand your
awareness, Respond
mindfully), 166
Minnesota Model, 192
Moderation Management (MM),
117–118
Mouyiaris, Nick, 51

naloxone, 71
naltrexone, 71
National Association for
Children of Alcoholics,
210
National Center on Addiction
and Substance Abuse,
Columbia University, 10
National Geographic, 64
National Institute of Mental
Health, 67

National Survey on Drug Use
and Health, 39
negative reinforcement, of
addiction, 49–50
neurotransmitters, 61–62.
See also brain
New Earth, A (Tolle), 244–245
New York Hospital-Cornell
Medical School, 56
nightclubs, avoiding, 173
Norstad, Frankie, 236

obsessive thinking, addiction
and, 51–52, 90–94
Off-Track Betting Corporation,
21
One Waverly Place (New York
City), 20
ORLAAM, 71
outpatient rehabilitation, 191.
See also therapy; treatment
OxyContin, 42–43

pain-body attacks, 245
painkillers, addiction to, 42–43
parents, 216–227
as addicts, 209
of adolescents, 66
communicating by, 220–221
consistency of, 222–227
gratitude taught by, 221–222
healing for siblings of addicts,
210–211
overcompensation by,
218–220

as overprotective, 216–217
role modeling, for addicts,
199–201
supporting addicted children,
195–199
of young children, 62
See also intervention
parties, avoiding, 173
passion, finding, 242–246
patience, importance of, 169
personality traits, 56–57
Phoenix House
on addiction rates, 5
author's experience with, 8–9,
31–32, 78
pornography addiction, 45
positive thinking, to prevent
relapse, 166–167
Power of Now, The (Tolle),
244–245
prescription drugs, addiction to.
See addiction; medication
present, living in, 245
proactive behavior, to prevent
relapse, 166–167
Promises (Los Angeles), 33
pro-social behaviors. *See* service
psychotherapy, 80–81, 91.
See also therapy

rapid eye movement (REM)
sleep, 170
recovery
different types of addiction
and, 47

program types, 77–84 (*See also*
    Hills Treatment Center)
Recovery Center, Washington
    Medical Hospital, 33
Red Bull, 196–197
relapse, 161–174
    author's experience with,
        8–9
    co-dependency and,
        164–165
    difficulty of, 161–163
    issues of, 86–89
    mindfulness practices for
        prevention of, 246–247
    preventing, 165–166
    rehabilitation discontinued
        and, 196
    therapy during, 183
relationships
    codependency and, 85–86,
        164–165, 205, 207,
        208–209
    moving away from family, 113
    problematic, as symptom of
        addiction, 50
    social pressure and addiction,
        58, 64–65
    See also families; intervention;
        parents
repetitive actions, as therapeutic,
    102–103
risk-taking
    addiction and, 56–57
    by teenagers, 64–67
Ritalin, 43

role modeling, for addicts,
    199–201
Rosenthal, Mitch, 31

Samuels, Barbara (mother)
    marriage of, 13–14, 15, 29, 91
    response to son's addiction,
        17, 19, 21, 30
Samuels, Bill (brother), 15
Samuels, Howard C.
    career of, 2, 33–34, 248–249
        (*See also* Hills Treatment
        Center)
    childhood of, 1–2, 13–15
    drug use by, 15–26, 27–31
    education of, 15, 16, 18–19,
        22, 27, 243
    rehabilitation of, 26–27,
        31–32, 111, 162
Samuels, Howard J. (father)
    business career of, 1, 13, 21
    death of, 31–32
    marriages of, 13–14, 15,
        29, 91
    political career of, 16–17, 18,
        19–20, 28–29
    response to son's addiction,
        19, 21–22, 24–26, 29–31
Samuels, Vicki (sister), 23,
    24, 29
Sander, Thomas, 235
self-medicating, 54
self-realization, 245
self-worth, 103
serotonin, 62

service
  benefits of, 235–239
  as hard work, 234–235
  ideas for, 239–240
  as therapeutic, 231–234
sex addiction, 45
shame
  gratitude instead of, 103–104
  issues of, 97–100
  writing in journals to
    overcome, 100–101
shyness, addiction and, 56–57,
    65–67
sleep, 169–172
Smith, Bob, 106
sober communal houses,
    118–120
SOBER (Stop, Observe, Breathe,
    Expand your awareness,
    Respond mindfully), 166
sobriety, maintaining, 84,
    247–249
specialized support groups
  benefits and drawbacks of,
    83–84, 237–238
  list of, 115–117
"speedball," 40
spirituality. See support groups
sponsors, in support groups, 117
spouse, as addict, 206–208
stimulants
  addiction to, 43
  Red Bull as, 196–197
Suboxone, 71
substance abuse. See addiction

Subutex, 71
suicide, risk of, 199
support, providing, 195–199
support groups, 105–120
  Alateen, 114–115, 215
  Alcoholics Anonymous,
    106–114
  Heart of Recovery, 118
  Last Call, 117–118
  Moderation Management
    (MM), 117–118
  sober communal houses,
    118–120
  specialized groups, 83–84,
    115–117, 237–238
  sponsors, 117
  value of, 105–106
symptoms of addiction
  behavioral addiction,
    53–54
  preventing relapse and, 174
  recognizing, 53
  relationship problems and, 50
  teenagers and drug abuse
    warning signs, 180, 199

"T," 40
teenagers
  Alateen for, 114–115
  brain development of, 62–67
  drug abuse warning signs, 180,
    199
  treatment and consent issues,
    192
  See also parents

television addiction, overcoming, 96

temptation, avoiding, 173

Terry (McGovern), 67

tetrahydrocannabinol (THC), 37

therapy
  for adult children of alcoholics, 209
  effectiveness of, 7
  finding therapist for intervention, 182–185
  group therapy and private counseling, 82–84
  importance of, 59
  inpatient rehabilitation, 191–194
  mindfulness techniques, 166, 246–247
  outpatient rehabilitation, 191
  professional help for whole family, 212–215
  psychotherapy, 80–81, 91
  repetitive actions as therapeutic, 102–103
  selecting therapists, 78
  service as therapeutic, 231–234
  shame addressed by, 99
  staying in, to prevent relapse, 168–169
  wilderness therapy, 194–195
  See also intervention; treatment

"tina," 40

Tolle, Eckhart, 244–245

trazodone, 170

treatment
  addiction type and, 36
  for depression, 68
  heroin withdrawal and, 24
  medication for addiction withdrawal, 70–73
  overcoming denial for, 59–60
  See also Hills Treatment Center

Trexan, 71

Trophy Kids Grow Up, The (Alsop), 217

12-step programs, 121–160
  Alcoholics Anonymous, 106–114, 117, 245
  for family members, 114–115, 200, 212, 215
  intervention and, 183
  sobriety maintained with, 84
  sponsors, 117
  See also worksheets, for 12 steps

University of Missouri, 235

University of Washington, 166

Valium, 44

Vicodin, 42–43

video game addiction, 46

volunteering. *See* service

Washington Medical Hospital, 33

wilderness therapy, 194–195

willpower, 165–166
Wilson, Bill, 106–107
worksheets, for 12 steps
  Step One (admit
    powerlessness over
    addiction), 122–125
  Step Two (believe in Power
    greater than ourselves),
    125–128
  Step Three (turn will/life over
    to God), 128–131
  Step Four (moral inventory),
    132–137
  Step Five (admit nature of
    wrongs), 137–139
  Step Six (remove defects of
    character), 140–141

Step Seven (humility),
    142–144
Step Eight (will to make
    amends), 144–146
Step Nine (make direct
    amends), 147–150
Step Ten (personal inventory),
    150–153
Step Eleven (conscious
    contact with God), 154–158
Step Twelve (carry message to
    addicts), 158–160
writing, in journals, 100–101

Xanax, 44

Zyban, 71